THE WORLD'S WORST
CONSPIRACIES

THE WORLD'S WORST CONSPIRACIES

THE TRUTH THEY DON'T WANT YOU TO KNOW

MIKE ROTHSCHILD

SIRIUS

SIRIUS

This edition published in 2019 by Sirius Publishing, a division of
Arcturus Publishing Limited,
26/27 Bickels Yard, 151–153 Bermondsey Street,
London SE1 3HA

ISBN: 978-1-78950-932-8
AD007179UK

Printed in Singapore

Contents

Introduction

On 4 December 2016, a man named Edgar Maddison Welch walked into a Washington DC pizza restaurant, armed with an assault rifle. His motive wasn't robbery, nor was he working as a hitman. Welch, instead, had become entangled with a conspiracy theory known as 'Pizzagate' – the evidence-free accusation that the pizza place Welch entered was actually a secret hub of child sex trafficking, part of a ring of evil that ensnared top level Democratic Party politicians and celebrities.

Claiming he was there to 'self-investigate' what he'd read on fringe conspiracy sites like Reddit and 4chan, Welch fired three shots into the floor, one of which bounced into a wall and went into another room. Although the restaurant was full of people, nobody was hurt, and Welch

The Comet Ping Pong pizza restaurant in Washington DC, which conspiracy theorists alleged was the site of child sex trafficking.

was peacefully taken into custody. In June 2017, he was sentenced to four years in prison, expressing regret for his 'foolish and mistaken' actions.

Pizzagate was a uniquely 21st century phenomenon, a conspiracy theory driven entirely by online supposition and 'investigation', that becomes much more about proving itself than about explaining something difficult to understand. And it's far from the only one.

These conspiracies weave themselves into politics, pop culture, food, healthcare and media; driven by social media and the instant availability of internet 'research'. And they've become hugely influential in all of those circles. So we end up with a presidential election dominated by fake news, a Brexit vote influenced by bots and misinformation, an alternative medicine industry that makes tens of billions off sham cures and quackery, baby boomers falling victim to conspiracy theories and scams, and shooting victims harassed over their 'crisis actor' roles in supposedly faked attacks.

The modern era presents us with both classic conspiracy theories and brand new ones, feeding off each other and creating an alternative universe where the only things that happen are things that we're being lied to about.

Many people believe that the moon landings were faked. Belief in one conspiracy theory tends to make it easier to acknowledge the merits of others.

The migrant caravan filled with Honduran refugees makes a stop in Mexico. Belief that the Jewish George Soros was funding the caravan has fuelled anti-Semitic extremists.

And belief in one conspiracy theory begets belief in others. If you wonder what 'really happened' to John F. Kennedy or Martin Luther King, Jr., or think that the moon landings were fake, you'll probably also believe that the US government is faking mass shootings, or that Big Pharma is poisoning us to sell cures, or any number of other popular conspiracy theories of the past few decades.

You also wouldn't be alone. Far from it. A 2014 poll reveals that half of Americans believe in some kind of medical conspiracy theory, such as mobile phones causing cancer or the Food and Drug Administration suppressing natural cancer cures in service of Big Pharma. A 2013 Gallup poll found that over 60 per cent of Americans are sceptical of the 'official story' behind the JFK assassination, and according to a poll by Fairleigh Dickinson University, 63 per cent of American voters believe in at least one political conspiracy theory.

And this isn't just an American phenomenon. A 2009 study found that between 30 to 40 per cent of UK residents have at least some belief in conspiracy theories; while a staggering eight out of ten citizens of France believe in at least one conspiracy theory, according to a 2017 poll by the French think-tank Fondation Jean-Jaurès.

While for most people, these theories remain topics for idle discussion, a few true believers have taken conspiracy theories into a sparsely-populated, yet extremely dangerous realm of paranoia. They've become obsessed by proving the government is out to get them, that their food is full of toxins, that the Illuminati control every aspect of their life, that vaccines and GMOs are culling the population. And most importantly, that they know the truth and are awake, while the rest of us are asleep.

And a few take up arms against their imagined oppressors, such as Edgar Welch, or Robert Bowers, the gunman who murdered 12 people in a Pittsburgh synagogue, driven by the mistaken belief that Jewish financier George Soros was funding the migrant caravan approaching the United States from Mexico before the 2018 elections.

So are all conspiracy theories as baseless and fictionalized as these?

Many actually begin with a germ of real information – a real incident, a scientific phenomenon, an actual person. Then they're grabbed on to by the conspiracy theory community, who often use that real thing as the jumping off point for a fantastical world, full of exquisite detail but essentially unprovable assertions.

And why do they take off? What purpose do they serve for their believers? Mostly, conspiracy theories function as the natural extension of humans' ingrained need to seek patterns. They bring order to chaos, and attempt to explain what seems like it can't be explained.

The Kennedy assassination is a perfect example of this. John F. Kennedy was the most powerful man in the world, a handsome and wealthy war hero beloved by men and women alike. His killer, Lee Harvey Oswald, was a loser who had accomplished nothing, and was so inept that he couldn't even defect to the Soviet Union without eventually drifting back. It's simply unacceptable to us that a nobody like Oswald could kill a national icon like Kennedy. Yet the 'official story' is that Oswald assassinated Kennedy on his own, with no help. Hence, millions of Americans have taken to believing in conspiracy theories that not only was such a thing not possible, it didn't happen. It's an alternate explanation for events where the 'official' one is unpalatable or unbelievable.

This book features the worst, most harmful conspiracy theories of the last few decades. These are supposed plots that have driven people to violence, to alienating friends and family, to losing jobs, and to becoming ensnared in a culture full of sugar rushes.

Mostly, conspiracy theories function as the natural extension of humans' ingrained need to seek patterns. They bring order to chaos, and attempt to explain what seems like it can't be explained.

Each chapter will run down a conspiracy theory, describing what it is, where it came from, what evidence there is that it might be true and what debunks it. Consider each chapter as a short, easily digestible explanation for why an 'official story' about something is most likely the true one. Share them with people who believe, people who don't, and people who might be on the fence.

And ultimately, read them to understand that belief in conspiracy theories doesn't mean you're crazy or should be shunned from society – only that your brain is exercising its natural need to seek patterns in chaos. But sometimes, those patterns just aren't there.

ASSASSINATIONS AND MURDERS

Do the wealthy and powerful really kill anyone who gets in their way? More than five decades after the Kennedy assassination, why do 75 per cent of Americans still think Oswald was a patsy? Was a vast government plot to kill Martin Luther King, Jr. revealed in a civil court case? And just how many people have the Clintons had killed, anyway? Find out as we examine the conspiracy theories behind some of the most important killings in recent history.

President John F. Kennedy in the motorcade in Dallas, moments before his assassination on 22 November 1963.

The Kennedy Assassination

There is no more important event in modern conspiracy theory culture than the assassination of President John F. Kennedy on 22 November 1963. While conspiracy theories had been omnipresent in western life before that, from rumoured Catholic and Jewish plots to whispers of slave revolts, the shooting of President Kennedy put them on the TV screen of the entire world. Countless millions of people watched helplessly as the news reports poured in of Kennedy's death, and then of Kennedy's killer being shot dead live on television several days later.

While it took Dallas police just 70 minutes to find and arrest Lee Harvey Oswald for the assassination (time enough for him to shoot and kill a Dallas police officer), many people at the time believed that Oswald must have had help or been part of a bigger conspiracy. And more than five decades later, many people still believe it. According

The open-roofed car that carried Kennedy through Dallas in November 1963 offered little protection against would-be assassins. This has not stopped many from believing there must have been more to the shooting than the actions of Lee Harvey Oswald.

to recent polling, 75 per cent of people subscribe to some conspiracy related to the Kennedy assassination, even if they can't agree on which one. But no evidence has been revealed that has ever truly debunked the initial conclusions about the crime: Oswald acted on his own, with no conspiracy to support or control him, and that he left an easily-followed trail of evidence that pointed his way. So then why do people still believe that a conspiracy took down Kennedy? Of all the unbelievable things that have happened in modern history, why does the act of a lone gunman killing John Kennedy still seem to be the most unbelievable of all?

Lee Harvey Oswald is escorted by Texas Rangers through Dallas police headquarters two days after the assassination. He was killed shortly afterwards.

THOUSANDS OF BOOKS, DOZENS OF KILLERS

Conspiracy theories explain events that defy explanation – and the Kennedy assassination defies explanation like no other. John F. Kennedy was a beloved and wealthy war hero with a loving family and the power to do almost anything humanly possible. Meanwhile, Lee Harvey Oswald was a directionless drifter who accomplished nothing of note other than defecting to the Soviet Union, then leaving after a year. The very idea of Oswald killing Kennedy on his own seemed not just impossible, but offensive. A titan like Kennedy deserved more out of his death, something bigger and grander. As William Manchester, author of the

The Warren Commission, set up a few days after the assassination, concluded that Oswald, and only Oswald, was responsible for killing Kennedy.

Kennedy conspiracy-debunking book *The Death of a President* wrote to the *New York Times* in 1992, 'if you put the murdered President of the United States on one side of a scale and that wretched waif Oswald on the other side, it doesn't balance. You want to add something weightier to Oswald.'

It didn't help that the initial investigation, usually referred to as the Warren Commission, was hopelessly complex, dragging on for almost a year, and encompassing countless witnesses and secrets in its 888 pages. The assassination was full of untrustworthy suspects rolling over on each other for various crimes, both real and imagined, muddying the waters to the point where more investigations were conducted. A second government commission in 1976 determined that Kennedy's murder was probably part of a conspiracy – while being unable to figure out who made up that conspiracy, or how it worked. But Kennedy had many enemies, figures in government, the military, organized crime and worldwide communism that wanted him out of the way. Oswald was the perfect man to take the fall for their crime, (he even referred to himself as 'just a patsy,') and his murder several days later by small-time mobster Jack Ruby looked like a ham-fisted way to finish the job.

To help find a more palatable explanation for the disparity between killer and victim, conspiracy theories about the Kennedy assassination have spawned anywhere from 1,000 to 2,000 different books, positing widely different scenarios for who 'really' killed Kennedy. Likewise, so many people have been accused of pulling the trigger (author Vincent Bugliosi pegged the number of alleged assassins at 82 in a 2007 book), that it would literally be impossible for all of them to be guilty. What better way to obscure the identity of the real killer than by flooding the discourse with fakes and conspiracy theories? And all the while, the government has sat on countless pages of Kennedy records, classified and filed away for future generations to mine for the truth. Even Donald Trump, who championed the release of the bulk of the remaining JFK files in 2017, changed course at the last moment and declassified only a portion of the files – which revealed little new.

The Greek shipping magnate and second husband of Jackie Kennedy, Aristotle Onassis, was one of many people conspiracy theorists have accused of killing the president.

WHY NOT OSWALD?

Among those accused of the crime by conspiracy theorists are the FBI, the CIA, the Secret Service, the Italian Mafia, the Corsican drug trade, unidentified drifters and spectators hanging around the assassination site, Greek tycoon Aristotle Onassis, the Majestic 12 UFO investigation committee, the KGB, NASA, Fidel Castro, Cuban dissidents, various lone wolves and hired guns, Vice President Lyndon Johnson, the American far right, American drug lords, the military industrial complex, the Federal Reserve, the government of South

The Carcano rifle used by Lee Harvey Oswald. Oswald was a trained marksman, who could be expected to hit a target just 88 yards away.

Vietnam, a mysterious shadow government, the Israeli government, Kennedy's limousine driver, and even First Lady Jackie Kennedy. And Oswald? To these authors, he was either a paid killer, one man on one of several shooting teams, a fall guy who had nothing to do with the shooting, or a sap brainwashed by propaganda or drugs. But if one boils away all of the other conspiracy theories, ephemera and bias, only Oswald remains. And while it's much more palatable to believe Oswald was part of a grander conspiracy, there's nothing in the assassination itself that requires him to be. In fact, it's just the opposite.

Lee Harvey Oswald was a former Marine who had tested at the second highest level of rifle marksmanship. He had easily been able to obtain a World War II surplus Carcano rifle, a reliable weapon made in 1940, and that rifle was easily traced to Oswald after it was found on the sixth floor of the Texas Book Depository, where Oswald fired at Kennedy with nothing blocking his line of sight. Kennedy's car had no top or armour cladding, allowing bullets to easily pass through it. It was also only moving about 11 miles per hour, and its driver didn't speed up or swerve once the first shot was fired. Kennedy was just 88 yards from Oswald's firing position – less than half of the distance Oswald would have fired at during his Marine testing. Finally, while many conspiracy theorists claim Oswald wouldn't have had time to aim, fire and chamber a new bullet three times, analysis of the filmed record of the shooting shows eight seconds between the first and final shot. For an experienced marksman firing at a slow, unprotected and close target, this would have been more than enough time to get off three good shots. And even then, Oswald still missed once. But the two hits he scored were enough to kill the president, and alter the course of world history.

> *The roots of JFK conspiracy theories lie in the natural disbelief that a man like Oswald could kill a man like Kennedy. But that doesn't mean he couldn't do it – or didn't.*

The roots of JFK conspiracy theories lie in the natural disbelief that a man like Oswald could kill a man like Kennedy. But that doesn't mean he couldn't do it – or didn't. Nearly six decades of alternate

theories and conspiracy allegations haven't changed that, or offered a foolproof alternative to Oswald. In fact, re-creations and tests done both immediately after the shooting and recently confirm that Oswald would have had no problem making the fatal shot. We're simply left with a crime that's both explainable and unexplainable at once. And perfect fodder for conspiracy theories.

The Texas Book Depository offers a clear line of sight to the street which the presidential motorcade passed through.

The Assassinations of Malcolm X and Martin Luther King, Jr.

■ Civil rights leaders Malcolm X and Martin Luther King, Jr. both met violent ends via assassination at the age of 39, and both in what many continue to believe were conspiracies driven by the US government. Malcolm's death, via shotgun blast on 21 February 1965, did indeed come as the result of a conspiracy – he was killed by three members of the Nation of Islam, which he had recently left as a result of philosophical differences. In contrast, King's death, three years later in Memphis, came at the hands of an inveterate racist named James Earl Ray. Like many other assassinations of powerful figures, it's difficult to reconcile the power they held in life with the seeming randomness of their deaths. But unlike the assassination of John F. Kennedy, whose death was accepted as the work of one man by those closest to him, Malcolm and King's assassinations are seen as conspiracies not just by internet theorists, but by their closest family members. King's wife and children have long accused a nebulous government conspiracy of setting Ray up to take the fall for King's murder, while Malcolm's death has been the subject of a number of alternate claims and recanted confessions.

What's the truth about these two assassinations? Why do so many powerful people continue to insist that something more must have happened? And why are the claims given credence, when such claims are almost always written off?

THE DEATH OF MALCOLM X

Malcolm X was outspoken, aggressive, unabashedly Muslim and did not hesitate to employ violence, both in word and deed. But after leaving the Nation of Islam, he looked to be on the verge of embracing a more mainstream (and palatable) view of black liberation. It never happened. The events of the day Malcolm died, during a speech at the Audubon Ballroom in Harlem, were clouded by a number of factors. Malcolm insisted on little security for his events, and that the police take a standoff role, with just 20 NYPD members there. His bodyguards were there

Martin Luther King and Malcolm X meeting in 1964 as they wait for a press conference.

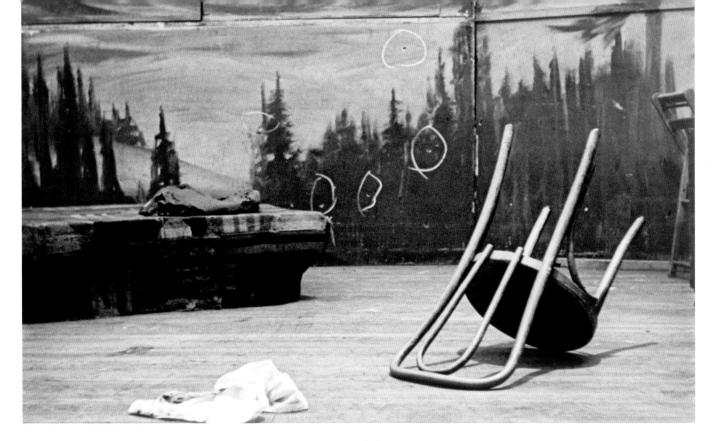

not to protect Malcolm, but to ensure the audience didn't get out of hand. As he began his speech, a disturbance broke out in the audience, and as Malcolm tried to calm it down, a man named Thomas Hagan rushed him and opened fire with a sawn-off shotgun. Two other men then shot Malcolm's body with pistols – for a total of 21 gunshot wounds. The aftermath turned into a melee, with audience members detaining and beating Hagan until the police arrived – taking their sweet time, according to allegations. Then, in the next few days, the NYPD arrested two more Nation of Islam members, Norman Butler and Thomas Johnson.

The entire matter seemed like the final act of a feud between Malcolm and his former ideological colleagues, but even though they were identified by witnesses, Butler and Johnson denied being at the Ballroom, and Hagan testified they weren't involved. Regardless, all three were quickly convicted and sent to prison.

In the next decade, information became public about the CIA's COINTELPRO project – an organized and well-funded effort to infiltrate and disrupt civil rights organizations. Possible CIA involvement with the Nation of Islam, along with the bizarre behaviour of Malcolm's security, the laxness of the NYPD and Hagan's shifting stories would all point towards Malcolm's death deserving a re-examination. But the case was never re-opened. Ultimately, until the government releases the extensive files it has on Malcolm X, it will be impossible to entirely debunk the conspiracy theories that the CIA had something to do with his death. But little has come out in the intervening decades that proves the three men convicted weren't involved, as Hagan had already confessed (then recanted), and the others were named by numerous witnesses.

The bullet holes from the shooting of Malcolm X at the Audubon Ballroom have been circled by the police, 1965.

Thomas Hagan was convicted for the murder of Malcolm X and claimed that he was the only one involved.

THE DEATH OF MARTIN LUTHER KING, JR.

Martin Luther King's death seems the more clear-cut case of a lone gunman. James Earl Ray was immediately fingered as the culprit, as a rifle and binoculars were found by the FBI across the street from the Lorraine Motel, where King was staying. Ray was already a convicted felon, so when his fingerprints were found on the rifle, it was easy to pin the crime on him. He was caught after a two-month manhunt, and pled guilty. But Ray recanted the confession, fired the lawyer who he claimed talked him into it, and insisted he was the patsy of a man named 'Raoul'. Unable to reconcile a common criminal like Ray as the killer, King's family embraced the story he spun, with his widow Coretta and several of his children talking up some grand government plot. And the

James Earl Ray was quickly blamed for the murder of Martin Luther King.

idea would only gain credence when the CIA's dirty deeds towards King were aired for the entire world.

The government's routine surveillance and harassment of King was shocking, even encompassing a conspiracy to get King to commit suicide through an extortion letter. In 1976, Congress conducted a second investigation of Ray, using forensic evidence and witness interviews to reach the same conclusion as in 1968 – Ray acted alone. All the while, Ray claimed he was innocent, though he was never able to explain who 'Raoul' was, what he was doing when King was shot, or why his fingerprints were on the rifle. Even his physical description of 'Raoul' changed over the years.

In 1993, the conspiracy got a new figurehead: a Memphis bar owner named Loyd Jowers, who appeared on TV claiming to have been the real shooter. Despite allegations that Jowers was simply trying to get a book deal, Coretta Scott King sued and won a judgement against him. In the aftermath of the trial, she announced that 'the civil court's unanimous verdict has validated our belief [...] that, in addition to Mr. Jowers, the conspiracy of the Mafia, local, state and federal government agencies, were deeply involved in the assassination of my husband. The jury also affirmed overwhelming evidence that identified someone else, not James Earl Ray, as the shooter, and that Mr. Ray was set up to take the blame.'

So did this trial prove that Ray was indeed the wrong man, and the FBI knew it for decades? Not quite. Jowers didn't testify at the trial, and for a good reason – he wasn't charged with anything. The FBI investigated Jowers for over a year and found that his story wasn't credible, so there was nobody to defend either him or the Justice Department. Ultimately, the jury quickly found Jowers and the government liable in absentia, and awarded King just $100 – the smallest amount possible. Jowers died soon after the trial, James Earl Ray died in 1998 and Coretta King died in 2006. King's children continue to insist that Ray was the fall guy for an unnamed conspiracy, but one that has never been proven to exist beyond one very flawed civil trial.

Ultimately, the conspiracies around both Malcolm and King's deaths revolve not around evidence, but belief – that these men were so important that no one person could kill them. There must have been something more involved – even if there's no real proof that there was. As former assistant district attorney John Campbell told National Public Radio in 2018, 'You just don't think that these powerful people, these people who are larger than life, can be killed by some nobody with a gun. You know, there has to be more involved. Well, sometimes there's not more involved.'

Coretta King, the widow of Martin Luther King, has been unwilling to accept the judgement that James Earl Ray was the only one to blame for her husband's death.

The Murder of Seth Rich

The 10 July 2016 murder of Seth Rich, a Democratic National Committee staffer working in their voter data section, became a focal point of conspiracy theories related to the 2016 US presidential election. The unsolved murder has led to countless articles, multiple investigations, several lawsuits and an unending and un-evidenced conspiracy theory: that Rich was the source of the hacked DNC emails released by WikiLeaks founder Julian Assange, showing members of the DNC insulting and colluding against Hillary Clinton's primary opponent Bernie Sanders.

Proponents see Rich's death as an example of the ruthlessness of the Hillary Clinton machine, a murderous and power-obsessed cabal that would do anything to grab the ultimate glittering jewel in the political crown – including killing someone who'd run afoul of it. But sceptics of the conspiracy theory take a different view: that Rich is being used as a pawn of the anti-Clinton lobby, that he had nothing to do with the Clinton campaign leaks, and that his death is merely a political prop for them to use, with his family or wishes being given no consideration.

So why did the unsolved killing of a Democratic staffer spark so much outrage and conspiracy mongering – and what does it mean for how we talk about politics?

> '*The conspiracy theories about the suspicious death of a DNC staffer right after the leaking of hacked DNC emails started at once.*'

A ROBBERY WHERE NOTHING WAS TAKEN

Seth Rich grew up in Omaha, Nebraska and moved to Washington DC in 2011. By 2014, he had joined the Democratic National Committee as Voter Expansion Data Director, designing programs to help voters find their nearest polling place. But according to published reports, Rich was going to be jumping from the DNC to take a more high-profile role with the Clinton campaign.

Rich left a Washington DC sports bar at about 1:30 on the morning of 10 July and began walking home. At one point, he was talking on the phone to someone, but the call ended abruptly. What happened over the next few hours isn't clear, but about three hours later, an automated gunshot recognition program picked up gunfire in an area between the bar and his apartment.

Seth Rich was found shot in the back twice. There were signs of a physical struggle on his body, and while nothing was stolen, his watchband was torn off. Rich was alive when found, and taken to the nearest hospital, but died shortly thereafter. He was unable to identify his attackers, and to this day, nobody has been taken into custody for the murder – which DC police view as a botched robbery.

The murder would have been just one of two dozen robberies that took place in the area where Rich was shot, a senseless tragedy that gave no closure to its victim or his family. But the timing of the killing, Rich's employer and the frenzied atmosphere of conspiracy theories and false plots spinning around the 2016 election would all ensure that this wouldn't happen for Rich.

The Democratic infrastructure had been plagued by hacks in 2016. One was the penetration of the DNC's email server, carried out by hackers using the name 'Guccifer 2.0.' These stolen emails were leaked in June and July of 2016, and included embarrassing conversations about Sanders, as well as uncensored discussions about the massive amount of money flowing into the campaign, what the *New York Times* described as 'bluntly transactional exchanges necessary to harvest hundreds of millions of dollars from the party's wealthy donor class.' The emails deeply embarrassed the Democratic establishment, and led to a number of resignations and a lingering rivalry between Clinton and Sanders supporters, some of whom vowed to never support the Clinton campaign.

The conspiracy theories about the suspicious death of a DNC staffer right after the leaking of hacked DNC emails started at once. One popular conspiracy site, the Russian-run 'WhatDoesItMean' published a tranche of meritless stories just days after the murder claiming that Rich had been on his way to meet with FBI agents regarding Hillary Clinton (in the middle of the night), only to be trapped and killed by a Clinton 'hit team.'

Mary Rich holds up a flyer with a photo of her son Seth as she seeks to discover who was responsible for his death.

Julian Assange added fuel to the fire of the conspiracy theorists when he mentioned that whistleblowers took significant risks when they sent material to him.

But the conspiracy theory really took off when WikiLeaks founder Julian Assange intoned in an 9 August interview that 'whistleblowers… take very significant risks' to get material to him. He then brought up Rich, though not by name, claiming 'then a 27-year-old, works for the DNC, was shot in the back, murdered just a few weeks ago for unknown reasons as he was walking down the street in Washington.' When asked if he was talking about Rich, Assange merely nodded and said 'we don't reveal our sources.' His site also put up a $20,000 reward for information about Rich's murder, an offer that would make no sense unless Rich had some kind of connection to the site.

Essentially, the conspiracy was that Rich had actually copied and sent the emails to Assange, tens of thousands of them over several months, and that Guccifer 2.0 was never real. The 'hack' was an inside job. And Rich paid for it with his life, with DNC chair Debbie Wasserman Schultz (who resigned because of the revelations in the emails) even hiring killers from the gang MS-13 to do the deed.

DEBUNKING THE CONSPIRACY

Seth Rich never had access to the emails leaked to Julian Assange. It wasn't part of his job, and a staffer at his level never would have been permitted to see such sensitive material. He wasn't a hacker, an expert programmer or someone who had ever been known to steal and leak anything. There's no evidence he took them, collected them or stole them.

None of the conspiracy theories about Rich and WikiLeaks ever established why he would undermine the party he was working for. By all accounts he was a fervent believer in the Democratic Party cause, and in Hillary Clinton in particular – to the

A member from the Mara Salvatrucha gang, also known as MS-13. Some conspiracy theorists allege that members from this vicious organization, which operates across North and Central America, were hired to kill Seth Rich.

point of being about to move to New York to work for her campaign. If he was a whistleblower, why would he do it? What triggered it? Nobody knows.

Not only do we know that Rich didn't hack or leak the emails, the public later learned beyond dispute that hacker Guccifer 2.0 was actually a front for Russian intelligence. In July 2018, Special Counsel Robert Mueller indicted over a dozen Russians for their roles in penetrating the DNC server. While it's unlikely any of them will ever see the inside of an American court, the indictment serves as a clear indication that the initial story of Russia's involvement was true, and Rich had no role whatsoever in the hack.

In fact, reporting by professional IT industry magazine *Computer Weekly* demonstrated that the leaked emails dumped by WikiLeaks were altered by the Russian hackers to include metadata pointing to Rich being the source of the emails. Essentially, they hacked the emails, then inflamed the conspiracy theories about the hack, including Rich's murder – all of which were wholeheartedly embraced by far-right media figures.

A street in Bloomingdale, Washington DC, the neighbourhood in which Rich was killed.

These conspiracy theories served no purpose other than to defame Democrats and push the 30-year-old conspiracy theory that Hillary Clinton is a stone cold killer. They didn't serve the Rich family at all, who begged leading figures on the right to stop propagating them. Rich's family even sued Fox News and several other conservative outlets who printed false statements connecting Rich to WikiLeaks.

Seth Rich was walking alone at night, distracted by his phone, in a neighbourhood prone to robberies. His body showed signs of a struggle, and of being shot in the back by an assailant who has never re-surfaced. No evidence has emerged in the last two years that changes the initial story, and no attempt to manipulate it has ever been backed up by evidence. His death remains an unsolved tragedy – and a lucrative gift for conspiracy theorists.

The Clinton Body Count

The rise of the anti-government militia movement in the early 1990s in the United States brought with it a conspiracy theory that lives on. Dubbed the 'Clinton Body Count', it's an ever-growing list of people somehow connected to Bill and Hillary Clinton who wound up suffering untimely deaths, either through an unsolved murder, suspicious accident, a fast-moving illness, or a 'suicide' that quite obviously was not self-inflicted.

There are several versions, some of which stretch on for hundreds of names. Some are people who were extremely close to the Clintons, most notably, former White House Counsel Vince Foster, who shot himself in the fallout from the scandal that eviscerated the White House

Conspiracy theorists accuse Bill and Hillary Clinton of killing a large number of people and covering up their murders.

Travel Office in 1993. Others had less tangible, but still real, links to the Clintons or their political machine, such as Democratic National Committee members, elected officials, fundraisers or security members.

Yet many others are random lawyers and reporters, or low-level government employees that never had any contact with the president. Some are street hoods from Little Rock. A few haven't even been conclusively proven to exist. And yet, the list continues to grow – even gaining new names in 2018, including a woman who died in a gas explosion in her home who was falsely claimed to be testifying against the Clinton Foundation, and a UN official who died in a weight-lifting accident.

The Clinton Body Count is intensely conspiratorial, rarely evidence-based and driven by leaps in logic that are often simply ludicrous. But it's also not surprising that it took off, given the heavy-handedness with which the Clinton administration took down several militia and anti-government groups, particularly the Branch Davidians compound after a long siege by the FBI.

It's also not as if powerful people don't have the ability to make their enemies disappear. Nor are the Clintons strangers to controversy, conspiracy and even allegedly illegal behaviour. Behaviour that they might want to cover up using the ultimate obscurant – murder. So did they?

Vince Foster, who shot himself in 1993 while he was the White House Counsel.

ORIGINS OF THE LIST

The first version of the Clinton Body Count list was put together by right-wing activist Linda Thompson, a lawyer who quit her job in 1993 to push

The Branch Davidian compound in Waco burns during the siege by federal agents. In a film about this siege called Waco: The Big Lie, *Linda Thompson put forward the theory of the Clinton Body Count.*

conspiracy theories. Thompson put it together based on research she'd done for an anti-Clinton film she'd produced, called *Waco: The Big Lie*, which accused Clinton of using ATF agents as hired killers to take out other agents during the Branch Davidians siege.

Thompson compiled the names of two dozen people that she believed had 'died suspiciously and had ties to the Clintons.' She freely admitted she had no actual evidence the Clintons killed these people, relying only on intuition that the media would find more here if it would only bother to dig. The list caught on in far-right American circles, being passed around on text-only BBS sites or via fax.

It made the jump into the mainstream in 1994, thanks to recently retired arch-conservative California congressman William Dannemeyer, who used Thompson's list as the spine of a letter he sent to Congress urging the body to investigate people in the orbit of the Clintons who died 'under other than natural circumstances'. The list was characterized by a US News and World Report article of the time as having 'serious deficiencies in corroborating evidence', and Congress declined to investigate the sitting president as being a serial murderer.

While the list was ignored by the mainstream media, it was embraced by the growing anti-Clinton conspiracy movement, stretching out to hundreds of names. Everyone from the elderly father of Hillary Clinton's physical therapist to the crew of a crashed military helicopter that Bill Clinton flew in once, were all said to be have been liquidated by the Clintons in a never-ending purge dedicated to consolidating their power.

The list even became grist for the 2016 election, with Donald Trump calling the suicide of Vince Foster 'fishy'. The Foster conspiracy also came up during the contentious confirmation hearing of Supreme Court Justice Brett Kavanaugh. And yet none of the names on it have ever been proven to have been killed by the Clintons. What's more, many people who actually have been thorns in the side of the Clintons, such as the conspiracy theorists who have made millions off them, are still alive.

WHY DOES ANYONE BELIEVE IT?

While theirs is the most famous, it's not just the Clintons who have a 'body count list' compiled in their name. Lists of suspicious deaths are common in conspiracy theory circles, with seemingly every powerful person and major event leaving behind a trail of mysterious suicides, crashes and murders.

The congressman William Dannemeyer brought the Clinton Body Count into the mainstream.

George W. Bush in the uniform of the Texas Air National Guard from his service days, c.1970. The body count list attributed to him includes commanders from the service.

Barack Obama has a death list with dozens of random names on it, including the health department official who released his birth certificate, Supreme Court Justice Antonin Scalia, a Hillary Clinton super delegate and a British banker. George W. Bush's body count list includes former Texas Air National Guard commanders, a conceptual artist and Commerce Secretary Ron Brown, who died in a plane crash – and is also on the Clintons death lists. And there are voluminous lists of dead witnesses to the JFK assassination.

It's not implausible that powerful people like the Obamas or Clintons would have a huge number of professional and personal connections. Bill and Hillary Clinton both had thriving careers in law and politics before Bill made it to the White House in 1992. Statistically speaking, some of these people are going to pass away – most naturally of illness, but a few unnaturally or before their time. If one were to take every person Bill Clinton ever met or who worked under him who died, they'd make a long list indeed. But that doesn't mean the Clintons *caused* their deaths, or even had any particular connection to that person that would necessitate their death.

This is the biggest logical fallacy at the heart of such lists – they lack motive. Why would the Clintons want some random dentist or state trooper to die, but Monica Lewinsky and Donald Trump to live? Beyond that, these lists make every death seem unnatural, even simple old age or protracted illness. If it was an accident, they always play up how suspicious it was, and toss in that the findings of investigators were 'alleged' or 'apparent' – even if they were obvious. They play up unimportant details as the most important thing, such as the lack of an autopsy on a person who dies of cancer, or how many times a person Bill Clinton met once 30 years ago was shot. And when in doubt, they just lie. Say a person committed suicide via two shots (the most frequent claim about Vince Foster), or that a plane 'exploded' when it crashed in bad weather. It doesn't matter.

These lists work not because they're accurate, but because they're long. They mistake quantity for veracity – a common trope in conspiracy circles that makes them easy to believe, and hard to debunk.

Ironically, the one name that would be a slam-dunk for such a Clinton Body Count list is almost always absent from the ones circulating on the internet. An enemy of the Clintons who relentlessly hounded them with conspiracy theories and unfounded accusations – original list creator Linda Thompson herself, who died in 2009 of a prescription drug overdose. If the Clintons didn't order Thompson killed, why believe they ordered anyone else killed?

> *Lists of suspicious deaths are common in conspiracy theory circles, with seemingly every powerful person and major event leaving behind a trail of mysterious suicides, crashes and murders.*

The Death of Kurt Cobain

■ Conspiracy theories about the death of an individual usually have smaller motives than grand government plots, often money or covering up something that someone else doesn't want known, rather than power and control. But they're just as compelling, because they're more believable and involve fewer moving parts. At heart, they all have the same motive: explaining something that seems to defy explanation.

The death of Nirvana lead singer Kurt Cobain on 5 April 1994, falls squarely into that category. Cobain's band was at the height of its commercial and artistic power. In the process, Cobain had become wealthy, famous and inspired a legion of copycat bands. But he was also struggling with a profound heroin addiction, as well as intense stomach pain from an undiagnosed condition, and unhappiness about the band's creative direction. Finally, he was in a tempestuous marriage to fellow musician Courtney Love. Cobain's struggle with addiction, pain and depression finally culminated in his suicide, via a shotgun blast to the head in his Seattle area home, several days after he'd disappeared from a residential rehab facility. His body was found the next day, with a suicide note next to it, and the shotgun resting on his chest. The police report indeed found that Cobain had killed himself.

But a small and vocal group of conspiracy theorists allege that Cobain was murdered, either at the behest of Love, or possibly by the CIA. And they've spent over two decades trying to prove it, writing books, making documentaries and dredging up anyone who thinks Cobain's death might not have been self-inflicted. Is the truth about Cobain's death far darker than what we've been

Kurt Cobain killed himself at the height of his career. Unable to understand the suicide, many fans have turned to alternate theories.

led to believe? Or are the conspiracy theories doing what they usually do, trying to find a more palatable explanation for an event that makes no sense?

The most common theory put forward is that Courtney Love killed Cobain to obtain his money.

TWO POSSIBLE 'REAL' CULPRITS

It's common to believe that a person who commits a violent act, either murder or suicide, couldn't or wouldn't have done it. This is not empirical evidence that something didn't happen – merely that what the person was alleged to have done was out of character. Cobain's suicide did indeed seem out of character to people who knew him, even as his health problems worsened to the point where he had briefly been in a coma a month earlier due to an accidental overdose of painkillers. And so it didn't take long for theories to emerge that because suicidal ideation was out of character for Cobain, he could not have actually done it.

There are a slew of claims and counterclaims regarding Cobain's death, some supported by evidence, and some not. The most prevalent conspiracy theory is that Courtney Love was involved, usually by paying a hitman to kill him and stage it like a suicide. Her motive is thought to be money, and more specifically that Cobain was about to cut her out of his will. Its main proponent is private investigator Tom Grant, originally hired by Love to look into why Cobain had left his drug rehab – only to uncover evidence that Cobain had been planning to divorce Love. Backing them up are several high profile documentaries, one called *Kurt and Courtney*, which has on-camera testimony from a musician named Eldon Hoke claiming that Love offered him $50,000 to kill Cobain in a staged suicide; and *Soaked in Bleach*, whose makers Love sued to have its release stopped, and whose conspiracies were said to be endorsed by Cobain's own mother.

All of these claims rely on some basic assumptions: that Cobain was too high on heroin to actually be able to pull the trigger on the shotgun, that the gun had three shells loaded into it, that the suicide note makes no actual mention of suicide until the last few lines (which don't appear to be in the same handwriting), and that Eldon Hoke mysteriously died in an accident shortly after appearing to confess his role in the murder. Above all, they believe that Cobain's death saved Love from losing millions in a divorce – and that Love has taken no legal action against any of the conspiracy theorists who accused her of a conspiracy to murder her husband, because doing so would lay bare her true role.

As bizarre as these theories are, there's an even more outlandish one: that the CIA murdered Cobain because his far-left politics had made him a liability. Just weeks after Cobain's death, Seattle radio host Richard Lee released a video series called *Kurt Cobain Was Murdered*, alleging government involvement in his death. Love herself seemed to echo this, telling news website *Hollywood Inquirer* that not only did she believe the CIA killed Cobain, but his drug overdose the month before his death was a botched attempt. 'The government had been trying to kill him for months, and I think they finally got him,' Love told the site. 'Kurt was murdered, and the CIA is behind it!'

A poster for the film Soaked in Bleach *(2015), which suggested that Cobain's death was not a suicide.*

SMELLS LIKE CIRCUMSTANTIAL EVIDENCE

Every single murder theory has problems. Many are simply based on the desire to not think that the people closest to Cobain missed his suicidal ideation. From a factual basis, the claim that Cobain was too high to kill himself ignores that Cobain had been a habitual heroin user for years, and likely had a high tolerance to the drug. The handwriting on the last few lines of the suicide note has never been proven to have been written by someone else, merely by someone in a different state of mind than the rest of the note. Many of the other details about the suicide cited by conspiracy theorists, such as the number of shells in the shotgun, an unusual brand of cigarettes found near Cobain's body and the lack of usable fingerprints on the gun, are either not relevant or not presented accurately. The 'endorsement' by Cobain's mother of conspiracy film *Soaked in Bleach* comes not from her, but from a divorce suit filed two decades later against Love and Cobain's daughter.

There's little hard evidence that Cobain and Love were actually about to split up, despite accusations from people with second and third-hand knowledge. Tom Grant claims to have spoken to Cobain's lawyer, and said she told him Cobain had planned to disinherit Love, but this conversation has never been confirmed to have taken place – just one of a number of pieces of evidence that Grant has claimed to have found, but never presented. And Eldon Hoke, who claimed to have been paid by Love to carry out the killing, did indeed die, after a drunken collision with a train. Finally, the supposed interview Love gave to the *Hollywood Inquirer* never took place, and the website is a fake news publication designed to scam clicks out of gossip-hungry readers.

Kurt Cobain was a habitual heroin user. Some have suggested that this would have made him unable to pull the trigger on the shotgun.

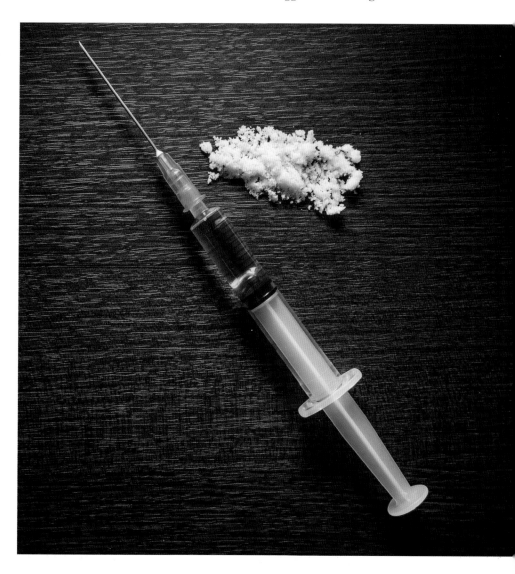

It's easier to believe that Kurt Cobain was murdered than took his own life. One explanation allows us to be angry at someone else, and the other forces us to confront the darkness in Cobain. The people closest to Cobain, including Love, his bandmates and his father, have all accepted that the death was from a suicide. Even the filmmakers of the Cobain conspiracy documentaries couldn't bring themselves to call it a murder, only a suicide with conflicting details. In the end, the tragedy isn't that Cobain was killed, but that he was sick and depressed enough to kill himself without anyone stopping it. And that's not a conspiracy, just the variance of human frailty.

SECRET ORGANIZATIONS

They're impossibly powerful, incredibly wealthy, untouchable by the law and, most importantly, you can't join them. From the New World Order to the Illuminati to the shapeshifting lizard people from Sigma Draconis who came to earth and pretend to be our leaders, here are some of the most important and shadowy secret societies said to be pulling the strings on world events. Cross them at your peril!

The Taschenbergpalais Hotel in Dresden served as the 2016 meeting place for the annual conference of the shadowy Bilderberg Group.

The Bilderberg Group

Take a small group of world leaders, sequester them in a luxury hotel surrounded by men with guns, keep their meetings shrouded in secrecy, and do it year after year. What do you end up with? A conspiracy theory about the elite getting together to talk about all of the horrible things they're going to do to the rest of us.

This is the crux of the Bilderberg Group, a small and ever-changing roster of notables in politics, business, academics and culture that meets yearly to discuss global issues. The group first met in 1954 at the Bilderberg Hotel in Oosterbeek, Holland to discuss the rise of anti-Americanism in Western Europe. It was comprised of one conservative and one liberal from each invited country, with the discussions informal, non-binding and, above all, secret. Since that first discussion, a steering committee has invited about 120 people to a different location for a weekend of conferences, held under Chatham House Rules, where any attendee of the meeting is free to use information from the discussion, but is not allowed to reveal who said it. As the leaked notes from one meeting put it, 'all participants spoke on an absolutely personal basis without committing any government or organization to which they might belong. In order to facilitate complete frankness, the discussions were confidential and no representatives of the press were admitted.'

While the actual discussions at Bilderberg Group meetings aren't disclosed, the list of attendees is. Among the luminaries to attend at least one Bilderberg meeting have been Bill Gates, Jeff Bezos, Angela Merkel, almost every modern British Prime Minister, Hillary and Bill Clinton, Henry Kissinger, multiple members of the Trump administration, Emanuel Macron, Prince Charles and countless other important and powerful people.

'SECRET LOBBYING FOR AN ANTI-DEMOCRATIC EUROPEAN SUPERSTATE'

Conspiracy theorists see the Bilderberg meetings (which haven't been held at the Bilderberg Hotel since the first year) as the most powerful people in the world

The Bilderberg Hotel in Amsterdam, where the group met for the first time in 1954.

talking about things they don't want anyone else to know about. The anti-Bilderberg faction has counted among its number Timothy McVeigh, 1999 London bomber David Copeland, Fidel Castro, conspiracy theory expert Alex Jones, American arch-conservatives and Osama Bin Laden. Those opposed to the Bilderberg Group describe conversation topics as nothing less than how to build a socialist uber-European government – or even worse, a one-world government devoted to crushing all opposition against it.

The popular conspiracy website Collective Evolution claims that Bilderberg is made up of 'a small group of people and the corporations they run [who] completely control all aspects of human life', and charts out the links between Bilderberg participants and pretty much everything else imaginable. Another highly-viewed conspiracy site, GlobalResearch.ca, cites a 'Bilderberg wish list', including 'centralized control of world populations by "mind control"', 'a New World Order with no middle class, only rulers and servants', 'a zero-growth society without prosperity or progress, only greater wealth and power for the rulers', and a 'global welfare state where obedient slaves will be rewarded and non-conformists targeted for extermination'.

The Bilderberg Group meetings are also lumped in with other conspiracy theorist touchstones like the Illuminati, Skull and Bones Society, Trilateral Commission, the Freemasons, the New World Order and the Council on Foreign Relations. While their relationships to each other are a Venn diagram of accusations, at heart, they're all believed to desire a cashless society ruled by mass socialism, culled with genocide or eugenics, and where our rights are taken away in exchange for

Angela Merkel and Bill Gates shake hands. Both have attended meetings of the Bilderberg Group.

The leading conspiracy theorist Alex Jones gives a speech in July 2016. He has regularly denounced the Bilderberg Group.

security from threats they've created. There are long lists of quotes from prominent Bilderberg attendees, such as Bill Gates appearing to claim he wants to use vaccines to cull the population, to Henry Kissinger spouting off about aliens landing on earth.

And all of this is done without any accountability to the people or access to the press, in luxury hotels surrounded by armed guards, razor wire and even helicopters. As David Rockefeller was reported to have said at the 1991 Bilderberg meeting, 'It would have been impossible for us to develop our plan for the world if we had been subjected to the lights of publicity during those years.' Enterprising journalists are constantly prevented from reporting on meetings, with heavy security harassing reporters who try to get close, and a few long-time Bilderberg chroniclers even being arrested. As the theory goes, if Bilderberg members were not conspiring to do us harm, then they wouldn't meet in secret. Only people with something to hide feel like they have to hide what they're doing.

> *'It would have been impossible for us to develop our plan for the world if we had been subjected to the lights of publicity during those years.'*
>
> DAVID ROCKEFELLER

BANAL MEETINGS OF IMPORTANT PEOPLE

There's little separating the conspiracy theories about the Bilderberg Group from those about any other elites, except that we actually know something about them. The list of attendees is published yearly, as are the locations of their meetings. They may have a lot of security around, and not want reporters writing about it, but that's far more likely due to the unofficial and unbinding nature of the discussions. And those discussions are useful as a way to safely workshop new ideas and strategies, with participants routinely praising the open and secure exchange of ideas. At the least, Bilderberg functions are nothing more evil than a 'supper club for the rich and powerful', as one British journalist put it.

Beyond that, we actually do know at least some of what's been discussed at individual Bilderberg meetings. WikiLeaks has published official reports from a number of meetings from the 1950s and 60s, along with a few from the 1980s. And far from being secretive discussions of who will be destroyed next, the topics are aggressively normal, even banal. For example, the notes of the 1958 meeting in Turkey contain discussions about how the west regards China, the future of NATO, increasing cooperation with the US, and early notes on economic unification in Europe. The meeting in Cannes in 1963 had discussions about the recently concluded Cuban Missile Crisis, France's rejection of England joining the European Economic Community, criticism of outsized American military spending, and fostering trade with the developing world. And the 1980 meeting notes, from Aachen, Germany, contain frank talk about the alliance between the United States and Western Europe, observations about Iran, ruminations on the SALT nuclear arms treaty, whether or not European nations should join the American boycott of the 1980 Moscow Olympics, and how NATO should regard future Russian aggression.

The discussions are frank and not always complimentary, but are able to take place because the speakers know they'll be kept anonymous. In keeping with Chatham House Rules, points made during discussions are written out in detail, but given little or no attribution. Commenters are referred to as 'a Portuguese speaker', or 'a French participant belonging to the government majority group', or simply 'one participant'. Nobody is making any decisions, giving any orders, or putting their country in an untenable position. There are certainly no references to total domination, mass killing, world government, or anything else conspiratorial. The need for secrecy goes hand in hand with the nature of the meetings, and any large enough gathering of powerful people is going to have outsized security.

Despite the protests, intrigue, conspiracy theories and secrecy, the Bilderberg Group is an important tool for fostering international relations and finding new solutions to difficult problems. And if it were used for anything truly horrible, its members probably wouldn't be so open about it.

Protesters march in Telfs, Austria, as the Bilderberg conference is held in their town in June 2015.

The Illuminati

■ Conspiracy theorists obsess about ancient, world-controlling secret societies, full of rich and powerful titans, pulling the strings on the rest of us. And there might be no secret society more ancient, more powerful and more controlling than the Illuminati. Paradoxically, it's also the most famous, least impactful and, ultimately, most misunderstood of all the supposed secret societies. Like many other conspiracy theories, there is a grain of truth to some of these accusations, in that there was a historical Illuminati. And it was crushed just as its power was beginning to grow. But it has no relation to the modern conception of the Illuminati – only to old stereotypes and fears of the unknown.

THE OLD NEW WORLD ORDER

According to over two centuries of accusations, made in everything from self-published pamphlets to Twitter, the Illuminati is the centuries-old cabal that controls every aspect of our politics, finance, culture, entertainment and economics. Its bloodlines include generations of world leaders, religious icons, titans of industry and bankers; as well as an ever-growing roster of musicians, actors, sports figures and internet celebrities, many of whom are merely pawns of the Illuminati, mind-controlled to espouse its beliefs to the uneducated masses.

And if something nefarious happens somewhere in the world, it's a good bet that the Illuminati made it happen, for a reason only known to them. Assassinations, currency manipulation, wars staged to sell arms to both sides, foreign coups, empires rising and falling, and even man-made disasters? All in the playbook of the Illuminati.

None of this happens in a vacuum. Pattern-seeking is an essential element of human thought, looking for ways to predict when the next predator will jump out of the bushes, or trying to figure out that if we don't feed and water our crops, we die. People desperately need to believe that things happen for a reason, that there's meaning in the events

The all-seeing eye shown on the back of the American dollar bill has become the universal symbol of the Illuminati.

of our lives, and not just random events cascading on top of each other. We need someone or something to be in control. And for a long time, that was the Illuminati.

So what are the Illuminati said to control? Virtually every major event of the last few centuries, starting with the French Revolution, moving through the Napoleonic and World Wars, peaking with the Kennedy assassination, and continuing through the 11 September attacks. They keep an iron grip on politics, starting wars to get their way. Or as one popular conspiracy book, *Bloodlines of the Illuminati* puts it, once you are awake to the Illuminati, 'wars between kings no longer appear as wars between elite factions, but contrived wars to control the masses by their greedy elite masters.'

Naturally, they jealously guard their wealth and power, killing anyone who opposes them, rigging economies to ensure their empires expand, and inserting secret brainwashing messages into entertainment and literature to stealthily let us know that they are in control. Every major world politician and titan of industry has a blood relation to the Illuminati, from the Rockefellers to the Roosevelts to the Rothschilds.

Not only does the Illuminati have its hooks into virtually every aspect

The French Revolution, along with many other major historical events, has been attributed to the machinations of the Illuminati.

Adam Weishaupt founded the Illuminati in Bavaria in 1776.

The Owl of Minerva, representing wisdom was the insignia chosen by the first Illuminati.

of our society, they're allied with the Freemasons, another shadowy cabal full of secrets and symbols. They've got links to the New World Order, the supposed one-world government conspiracy theory of the 1990s. They reinforce their hold over us by putting symbols on our money (the 'all seeing eye' on the US dollar bill), monitor us through the National Security Agency, control our weather, health and food; and send out an endless roster of celebrities to dazzle our unthinking minds with displays of loyalty and human sacrifice.

As Alex Jones has said of the Illuminati, the shadowy group is no less than 'an intergalactic invasion into this space through people. I'm telling you, it's what all the ancients said. It's what they warned of. It's what we're dealing with. They're demons! They're frickin' interdimensional invaders, OK?'

'THE HIGHEST POSSIBLE DEGREE OF MORALITY'

The real, historical Illuminati movement was founded on 1 May 1776 in Bavaria, by Adam Weishaupt, a professor of Canon Law at the University of Ingolstadt. He was also an ardent foe of the doctrinal and conservative Catholicism of the Jesuits who ran the college.

A liberal secularist, he rankled at the influence of Catholic doctrine over philosophy and the sciences, as well as its control of the Bavarian monarchy. Weishaupt and those who agreed with him went underground, and after being rejected by the Freemasons, they formed their own secret society, borrowing some of the Freemasons' rank system and terminology, but with a far more liberal ideology – one devoted to equality, the embrace of new ideas and fighting the abuses of a corrupt state and the dogma of a controlling Church.

It took two years for the group to settle on the name 'Order of Illuminati', selecting for its logo the Owl of Minerva, the Greek symbol of wisdom. In those early years, it measured its membership in single digits, and only about 650 men ever obtained even one of the three degrees Weishaupt's society offered (the Freemasons have 33 degrees). By the early 1780s, it was still just a debating society, as Weishaupt and a few acolytes espoused anti-religious and pro-equality ideas to a few dozen ardent believers. They also poached members of other Masonic lodges, and while they later claimed to have about 2,500 members in total, it was probably far smaller.

By 1785, the group had found a few powerful benefactors, and was expanding into other cities and universities. Alarmed by the expansion of these anti-state, anti-Church teachings, and driven by the general anti-secularism of the times, Duke of Bavaria Charles Theodore banned all secret societies, sending infiltrators in to root them out. The Duke's tightening net sent Weishaupt fleeing, ending the group after less than ten years.

It wasn't until decades later that several popular conspiracy theory books became the foundation for an argument that the Illuminati not only hadn't been broken by Charles Theodore but was far more powerful than anyone imagined. These books were particularly embraced by anti-Masonic conspiracy theorists, and blamed their ideas for the carnage of the French Revolution – a movement which shared many philosophical traits, but had an entirely different method of accomplishing them.

Those books offered no real evidence that the original Illuminati society even had goals of world domination and enslavement of the masses. In fact, Weishaupt saw the society's goal as 'to attain the highest possible degree of morality and virtue, and to lay the foundation for the reformation of the world by the association of good men to oppose

Charles Theodore, the Duke of Bavaria from 1777–99, banned all secret societies in his territory, including the Illuminati.

the progress of moral evil.' As Thomas Jefferson wrote in 1800, 'Wishaupt [sic] believes that to promote this perfection of the human character was the object of Jesus Christ. That his intention was simply to reinstate natural religion, & by diffusing the light of his morality, to teach us to govern ourselves.'

Neither of these quotes sound like the modern perception of the Illuminati as a war-starting, string-pulling cabal. They sound much more like historical perceptions of the Jewish people, who were tagged with many of the same conspiracy theories that the Illuminati had applied to them. Nonetheless, the Illuminati became the fodder for countless conspiracy theories, books, games and internet memes.

Weishaupt's society was intellectual, egalitarian and moralistic. It was also small, young and had little influence in Bavarian society. And once that started to change, it was crushed. Whatever other secrets it held were made public at the time. There's no real evidence that any parallel or subsequent Illuminati has had any influence on any events since.

The Reptile Elite

Reptoid. Reptilian. Draconian. Saurian. Lizard men. Anunnaki. Lizard aliens. The Reptile Elite. While they go by many names, all describe reptile-like aliens from a faraway star that have infiltrated earth's governments, taking human form to manipulate events on the planet. By taking human beings and harvesting us for scientific information (through devouring our flesh and blood, naturally), the reptilians have wormed their way into our society, taking control of our nations, paving the way for their eventual invasion – and our conquest.

Reptile-like aliens are a stock trope of both conspiracy theories and science fiction, usually given shape-shifting and mind controlling powers, and almost always bent on doing evil to humans. But they're also a huge part of ancient mythology, literature, folklore, pseudo-history and even video gaming. Many different cultures have depicted winged serpents, man-snakes and lizard people as part of their creation myths. With so many depictions of reptile aliens, and so many deeds ascribed to them, it can be difficult to keep track of what is an actual, legitimate legend about leathery visitors from the sky, and what's just the bizarre opinions of a fringe author.

So are reptoids real? Are they walking among us, wearing the skin of Queen Elizabeth, Barack Obama, Warren Buffett, Hillary Clinton and other leaders? Do they have underground bases around the United States? Are they waging a war with other, equally powerful aliens? And have they been planning their conquest for thousands of years?

Are there secretly reptilian aliens hiding beneath the faces of some of the world's most powerful people? That is what some conspiracy theorists would have you believe.

TWELVE FEET TALL, BLOOD-DRINKING SHAPE-SHIFTERS – OR NOT

The longer a conspiracy theory sticks around, the more irrelevant details it picks up. So any dive into the mythology around the reptilian alien theory becomes bogged down in fake alien hierarchies, biology, geology and history. Some of it intertwines with ours, some of it spirals off into digressions about angels, gods and vast intergalactic empires. The deeper one goes, the more it all seems like a mash-up of *Star Trek*, the Bible and heavily-trod UFO mythology. But little of it was simply made up on the spot. Reptilian humanoids have been part of pop culture for nearly a century, making one of their first literary appearances in the fiction of Conan the Barbarian creator Robert E. Howard in the late 1920s. But it was prolific conspiracy theorist David Icke who first cemented the idea of a powerful Reptilian Elite pulling the strings on the human race in his 1998 book *The Biggest Secret: The Book That Will Change the World*.

The basics of Icke's 'biggest secret' are that reptile aliens from the star Sigma Draconis (18.8 light years from earth) came to our world in ancient times. Seeing the planet as an opportunity for plunder, they used their shape-shifting abilities to interbreed with humans, spawning dozens of royal bloodlines, and quickly becoming our rulers. They now make up virtually every royal dynasty, most wealthy families, legendary cultural figures, bankers, great scientists and nearly three dozen presidents. They are said to control unimaginable wealth, power and military might. And they manipulate all of it in the service of fighting their own war, against the beings colloquially known as the 'grey aliens' – a race of diminutive,

Barack Obama and Warren Buffet are two of the supposed members of the reptile elite.

David Icke is the most well-known advocate of the reptilian conspiracy theory.

The Hall of Pontifical Audiences in Rome is shaped like a snake's head, supposedly providing evidence of the conspiracy.

large-eyed humanoids from Zeta Reticuli, located about 39 light years from earth.

Icke's reptilians were the culmination of years of his exploration of new age spirituality, alternative medicine, ancient legends, Christian eschatology and prophecy. They were also derided as fascist, anti-Semitic and completely insane. And they skyrocketed in popularity as Icke wrote about them more, and further developed his mythology. Books like *Children of the Matrix, The David Icke Guide to the Global Conspiracy: And How to End It* and *Human Race Get Off Your Knees*, spilled out more details about the lizard-human hybrids that controlled our world, exactly what they'd done to us, and how we had to free ourselves from their clawed grip.

'They're feeding off humanity,' Icke told *Vice* in 2012. 'They're turning humanity into a slave race. They demand human sacrifice – that's where Satanism comes in. They feed off human energy. They feed off the energy of children.' Other conspiracy theorists ran with the concept, and soon there was an ecosystem of websites and books about the horrid doings of the lizard people, and about their war with the grey aliens. One site posits that the Hall of the Pontifical Audiences, where the Pope has held large gatherings since the early 1970s, is shaped like a snake's head; while other conspiracy sites add incomprehensible details to the grey/reptoid war, even positing a peace treaty between the greys and the United States. A video on the YouTube channel 'Reptilian Resistance' got over 3.2 million views showing how a Secret Service agent protecting Barack Obama is actually a lizard alien. Icke counts *The Color Purple* author Alice Walker and mainstream right-wing media figures as admirers of his. And Icke himself has sold over half a million books in just the United States and England.

It's clear that despite its outlandishness, the Reptilian Elite conspiracy theory has caught on with at least some segment of the population. But what is it that they really believe?

'NOT A JEWISH PLOT'

Icke's reptilian elite conspiracy theory feels novel, but it's a mishmash of UFO abduction stories, urban legends, pop tropes and old conspiracy theories. There's little in Icke's books that can't be gleaned from other sources. Lizard-like beings populate the mythology of ancient Greece, Rome, China and Egypt. There are stories as far back as the 1930s of lizard people being on our earth and digging vast tunnels, along with more modern pop depictions of reptoids, like a 1973 episode of *Doctor Who* featuring lizard aliens called Draconians, the mini-series *V* (which has almost the same plot of lizards in human disguises) and the lizard-like Gorn alien from the *Star Trek* episode 'Arena'.

Likewise, much of the mythology around the grey aliens, supposedly the sworn enemies of the reptilians, is pulled from alien abduction stories like that of Betty and Barney Hill from 1961, or the legends about the 1947 Roswell crash. And the 'bloodlines' element of the reptilians comes straight from mythology about the Illuminati. Icke even conflates the two at times, and the supposed membership and dirty deeds of the two are basically the same.

There's another aspect to the Reptile Elite conspiracy theory that can't be ignored: anti-Semitism. Icke claims not to be anti-Semitic, and has said that the reptoid conspiracy 'is not a plot on the world by Jewish people.' But his descriptions of the lizard elite as shape-shifting, blood-drinking and dedicated to conniving evil match up with classically racist descriptions of Jews. He has embraced Holocaust denial, calling *Schindler's List* tyrannical indoctrination that shows 'the unchallenged version of events.' And in his book *The Truth Shall Set You Free*, Icke lays out exactly who is to blame for all the world's woes, writing, 'I strongly believe that a small Jewish clique which has contempt for the mass of Jewish people worked with non-Jews to create the First World War, the Russian Revolution and the Second World War.'

The anti-Jewish sentiment that undergirds the Reptile Elite is common to conspiracy theories, where Jews are blamed for everything from supposed genocide to the flat earth movement. Icke didn't make it up, he merely found a new way to monetize it. Ultimately, his conspiracy theory isn't especially novel or unique, only compelling to people who want to find an alien explanation for human events that they don't like.

CHARLES EDWIN WILBOUR

Lizard-men commonly featured in mythology. Sobek, an ancient Egyptian god with a crocodile head, is one such example.

The Rothschild Banking Family

■ The Rothschild banking family (no relation to the author of this book) is the subject of countless conspiracy theories, rumours, accusations and slander. All harness one of the oldest hatreds in history, that of Jews, and combine it with the speed and truth vacuum that the internet provides. Among the accusations against the Rothschilds are that they control most of the world's money supply, are involved in dark rituals and devil worship, that they've manipulated the economies of almost every nation on earth, and have started countless wars while funding all of the participants – all to slake their limitless thirst for wealth and power.

But conspiracy theories aside, the Rothschilds do have a long history of successfully investing around the world. They also were, for quite some time, the most prominent face of Jewish wealth. And much of it has been done in secret, with huge amounts of money moving through mysterious corporations that are held only by family members. So what's the truth about the Rothschild conspiracy, and what's just conspiracy?

Mayer Amschel Rothschild was the founder of the extraordinarily wealthy and successful Rothschild dynasty.

'I CARE NOT WHO MAKES THE LAWS'

The Rothschilds amassed the world's largest private fortune in the 19th century, with a line beginning at dynasty founder Mayer Amschel Rothschild and continuing through his five sons, sent to the financial centres of Europe. The insular nature of the family gave it an aura of mystery and impenetrability. And in deeply anti-Semitic Europe of the 18th and 19th centuries, that's all it took for a parallel pseudo-history to be born.

According to various accusations, the Rothschilds control as much as 80 per cent of the money supply of the world, building a fortune through a ruthless investing, dark manipulation and massive rigging of world events. Much of the early lore about the Rothschild family concerns their role in the Battle of Waterloo, particularly Mayer's son Nathan. It became a legend in Europe that Nathan invested in both sides of the battle, fooling the rest of Europe into losing a fortune, and even quipping 'buy when there's blood in the streets, even if the blood is your own.' But the most famous quote of the Rothschilds comes from Mayer himself, long held to have remarked 'give me control of a nation's money supply, and I care not who makes its laws.'

The Rothschilds were said to have invested massively in both sides of the Napoleonic Wars, the American Civil War, the Franco-Prussian

War and World Wars I and II. When any leader got in their way, such as Abraham Lincoln or John F. Kennedy, the Rothschilds simply had them killed. They are said to control countless puppet leaders, including Hitler, born of Mayer's son Salomon and an Austrian housekeeper. The Rothschilds are even alleged to have orchestrated the Holocaust, to push for the founding of Israel.

The Rothschilds were said to have made their fortune by investing in both sides of the Battle of Waterloo.

Through it all, the Rothschilds have been buying up central banks around the world, with only a few outliers such as Iran, Russia and North Korea subject to a constant string of Western aggression. All of this market manipulation has given the Rothschilds a fortune that some conspiracy theorists peg at 500 trillion dollars. And it's invested in vast estates where the family delights in human sacrifice to Moloch, hunting people for sport, Satanic rituals, masked balls where no outsiders are allowed, and even cavorting with reptilian aliens. Any Rothschild member who objects is murdered through staged suicide, as the family consolidates its power and stamps out anyone who would get in its way.

MORE WEALTH THAN EXISTS ON EARTH

Conspiracy theories about the Rothschild family began almost as soon as Mayer Amschel Rothschild began building his fortune. As conspiracy author and sceptic Brian Dunning puts it, 'their history is perhaps largely responsible for the modern belief that Jews control the world's money supply.' In middle ages Europe, Jews were forbidden from owning property, and were often pushed into occupations considered 'inferior' or sinful, such as money-lending, tax collection and banking. In particular, Jews were allowed to do one critical thing Christians weren't: charge interest. This divide allowed Jews to amass large fortunes through lending and recouping interest, and keep it in their own banks, hiding and moving money as needed.

Wilhelm I of Hesse employed Mayer Rothschild as his personal banker.

The Rothschilds provided the funding for one of the most ambitious projects of the late 19th century, the building of the Suez Canal.

Mayer Amschel Rothschild excelled at this, building up enough of a fortune to do business dealings with the nobility of Germany. Rothschild supplied coins to the future Crown Prince of Hesse, Wilhelm, eventually becoming his personal banker, and investing Wilhelm's fortune to the point where he became the richest man in Europe. Mayer then acted as a go-between for England and Hesse in the hiring of mercenaries to fight in the American Revolution. By the time Napoleon invaded Hesse in the early 1800s, sending Crown Prince Wilhelm into exile, Mayer had already sent his five sons to the five major financial centres of Europe to continue expanding the rapidly growing family fortune.

By the 1900s, the Rothschilds had rescued the Bank of England from a liquidity crisis, were often called upon to stabilize struggling central banks, had financed the building of the Suez Canal, invested massively in some of the most desirable real estate in Europe, held diamond and mineral mines, and had vast sums of money invested in railroads, art, wine and asset management. But does this all add up to the '$500 trillion' amount that conspiracy theorists allege? No, because that number represents more money than the entirety of the gross domestic product of the world. The accusation that they control '80 per cent of the world's money supply' is also massively overinflated. Both of these numbers appear to have been made up, and have no supporting documentation. In fact, there is no individual Rothschild in the top 1,000 on *Forbes'* list of richest people.

Many of the conspiracy theories about the Rothschilds' history are based on wilful misunderstandings of complex concepts in banking. There are no 'Rothschild central banks', because a central bank is a government-owned financial instrument that sets fiscal policy and prints money, not a private institution. Nor did the Rothschilds 'take over' the Bank of England, as many conspiracy theorists allege, merely make a loan that was repaid. Nathan Rothschild did not manipulate the Battle of Waterloo to profit off both sides, while fooling

The Schloss Hinterleiten was one of many palaces built by the Rothschilds. In 1905 the family donated it to charity, reflecting a tendency towards philanthropy that continues to this day.

investors into thinking England had lost (a bit of folklore that comes from a Nazi-era movie). He merely was able to get the news of England's victory quickly, then bought British government bonds – correctly calculating that they'd spike in value. And there's no evidence the family has 'funded both sides' of every major war, nor that they have the wealth to do so.

The vast majority of the other accusations, such as Hitler being a descendent of the Rothschilds, or the family holding human sacrifices at their estates, or assassinating John Kennedy, are simply rumours created and spread by anti-Semites. Some originate with the Nazis, others with the modern internet conspiracy movement. Even the quote so often attributed to Mayer Amschel Rothschild, the one that casts the family as manipulators of world events for profit, is apocryphal, with no primary source.

The modern Rothschild family is still wealthy and secretive, but also philanthropic and vocal about the causes it supports. It's divided up between generations of members, with its original monopolies on lending long dissolved. Its estates have largely been sold off, its art given away. Much of the power it retains in the conspiracy community, then, comes thanks to the historical conspiracy theories about it, not anything it's currently doing.

The New World Order

■ Many conspiracy theories feature the power elite uniting to exploit those deemed to be 'useless eaters' – those requiring help from society but giving nothing back. The one known as the 'New World Order', popular in the 1990s but still very much a going concern in the conspiracy community, is more plausible than most because it has roots in very real geopolitical events. Politicians and statesmen have continuously been trying to remake the 20th century world in their image, tossing out the old ways of war and ushering in a new order based on peace and equality. Some of the greatest minds of the last hundred years have tried to push society towards what they deemed a 'new world order', and these proposals have been twisted and reinterpreted by conspiracy theorists as something much darker – moving the planet away from freedom and self-determination and towards globalization and central control. Mass surveillance, global government, the purging of dissenters, mind control, planned economies feeding into one socialist system, and even the fulfilment of biblical end times prophecies are all key components to the conspiracy theory version of a 'new world order'.

While some of what the New World Order conspiracy theory posits is interchangeable with other theories, it also stands on its own as a unique entity with a long history. Are we really forever standing at the precipice of world government and socialist slavery?

Woodrow Wilson helped create the idea of a 'new world order' through the 'Fourteen Points' he put forward after the end of World War I.

TOWARDS A NEW WORLD ORDER

There is a sizable difference between what politicians and authors have generally referred to as 'a new world order' and the specific proper noun 'the New World Order' of conspiracy theories. The first has no specific definition, while the second does. Statesmen have long sought to use international traumas like the World Wars as the jumping off point for a more peaceful and less atavistic global society. It was President Woodrow Wilson who first codified the idea of a new world order with his call for putting international cooperation ahead of nationalistic goals. Wilson's 'Fourteen Points' were a blueprint for a world ravaged by the Great War, where disputes could be settled without violence,

including the creation of a 'general association of nations' that became known as the League of Nations.

Despite their good intentions, the United States rejected Wilson's ideas, with Theodore Roosevelt calling the Fourteen Points 'high-sounding and meaningless', and another US Senator calling the proposed League of Nations 'treacherous and treasonable'. It would not be the last time that the concept of a 'new world order' was dismissed and insulted, with no less than Adolf Hitler referring to the League as a 'new world coalition' meant to cover for French militarism. Nonetheless, some versions of the Wilsonian new world order were revived again after World War II, leading to the United Nations, NATO and the International Monetary Fund.

But the most famous use of the phrase 'new world order' came in the aftermath of the Cold War. Sensing the opportunity to remake the world free of east vs. west aggression, reformist Soviet premier Mikhail Gorbachev told the UN in a June 1990 speech that 'For a new type of progress throughout the world to become a reality, everyone must change,' and that 'tolerance is the alpha and omega of a new world order.' His counterpart, US President George H. W. Bush echoed Gorbachev by telling a joint session of Congress that September that 'we

George H. W. Bush was another leading statesman to talk of the creation of a new world order.

Black helicopters loaded with armed government thugs have become the fearful image of the supposed New World Order.

can see a new world coming into view. A world in which there is the very real prospect of a new world order.' After Bush used the term, decades of conspiracies about some undetermined mass of power elites taking control of our world suddenly had a figurehead – and an agenda to be fought.

BLACK HELICOPTERS AND WACO

To conspiracy theorists, the New World Order Gorbachev and Bush were proposing wasn't defined by tolerance or peace, but by naked lust for power. In his 2010 book *The New World Order: Facts & Fiction*, conspiracy theorist author Mark Dice defines the New World Order as 'the plan to create a socialist global government headed up by one world leader and a wealthy ruling class […] and render the rest of the world's population powerless.'

This wasn't new in conspiracy theory circles. Author Gary Allen had written several books using the phrase to label a globalist cabal working together to undermine the west. Other popular books in that same vein were John Stormer's *None Dare Call It Treason*, William Guy Carr's *The Red Fog Over America* and William Luther Pierce's *The Turner Diaries*. They all told of a powerful alliance of Communists, Jews and the government working to destroy everything dear about America. The concept was also popular with paleo-conservative groups like the John Birch Society, as well as Christian millennialist movements, spurred by Pat Robertson's hugely popular 1991 book *The New World Order*. Robertson mashed a generation of conspiracy theories together, putting everyone from the Freemasons to New Age practitioners to Wall Street bankers in a vast plot to enslave free people under the eye of a tyrannical world government. In the conspiracy crazed first years of Bill Clinton's presidency, New World Order fever was all over AM radio, the nascent internet, American churches and TVs, and books sold at gun shows and surplus stores. Talk radio hosts fretted about black helicopters and jackbooted FBI thugs, while anti-government militias armed up, Mulder and Scully tangled with conspiracies and monsters on *The X-Files*, and televangelists preached that societal collapse was only one UN initiative away.

It didn't help that the Clinton administration was involved in several incidents that New World Order believers saw as portends of things to come: the burning of the Branch Davidians compound in Waco, Texas;

and the shooting of Aryan Nation member Randy Weaver's wife and son by ATF agents. There were also multiple new laws seen as an unacceptable rollback of gun rights, including the Brady Handgun Violence Prevention Act of 1993, which mandated federal background checks and waiting periods, and the much-derided Assault Weapons Ban of a year later. But the crescendo of organized opposition to the New World Order came on 19 April 1995. Conspiracy theorists Timothy McVeigh and Terry Nichols were hardcore believers in the New World Order, and inspired by the disaster at Waco, they sought to fight back against what they believed was a local headquarters of the nefarious organization: the Alfred P. Murrah Federal Building in Oklahoma City. McVeigh and Nichols built a gigantic truck bomb, and McVeigh detonated it, killing 171 people, including a number of children. The uprising that the two men hoped to provoke never took place, and the anti-government militia movement was eviscerated by the FBI in the wake of the attack.

With that, belief in the New World Order suddenly became a lot less trendy and acceptable, with many believers moving on to other conspiracy theories – some related to the US government, and some not. But even though the idea of a named and organized 'New World Order' has fallen out of favour in the movement, the concept of a world-controlling, string-pulling cabal is still very much a going concern. The modern idea of the deep state relies on the same combination of end-of-the-world prophecy, fear of government overreach, relentless fear-based grifting, and cabalistic bankers engineering world events that the New World Order did. And while that movement was stopped by the backlash to the Oklahoma City bombing, the modern deep state has had no such incident to dim its popularity. At least, not yet.

The ruins of the Murrah Federal Building in Oklahoma City. Timothy McVeigh and Terry Nichols bombed it because they believed it was one of the headquarters of the 'New World Order'.

POLITICAL CONSPIRACIES

Staged mass shootings to instil fear and take away gun rights; eradication of the poor and unwanted through drugs and disease; vast international plots to strip us of our rights to travel, freely associate and play golf while shoving us into urban ghettos. If there really is a deep state at the centre of western politics, these are just a few of the nefarious conspiracies they'd use to make sure we don't cast off our chains.

Robert Mueller, former FBI director and the Special Counsel investigating Russian interference in the US presidential elections, walks to a meeting in June 2017.

The Deep State

■ Since taking office in 2017, President Donald Trump has dealt with a sustained wave of investigations, leaks and turnover on his staff. While seeming to be a by-product of an administration that entered office with little experience or understanding of the role of government, some believe it to be a highly-organized and funded opposition – a kind of double government or shadow organization, dedicated to preventing or defeating everything Trump has tried to do.

The term most often applied to this supposed organized opposition is 'deep state'. And while definitions as to what and who exactly make up the deep state vary, its existence is all but a certainty to conservative pundits, who describe it as 'an army of bureaucrats' working with leftists in the mainstream media and banking to execute an anti-Trump coup. It's unelected, unaccountable and answers to the most powerful Trump enemies in the political sphere.

Shadowy states-within-states are common in countries with heavy-handed control by the military or a dictator. But what is the American deep state? Is it even real? Or can the Trump administration's various stumbles and legal woes be attributed solely to the chaos at the highest levels of the administration – a constant roil of scheming and bad press that's cost numerous Trump officials their jobs, and kept the Trump White House under the constant eye of investigation?

> *The concept was first articulated in President Dwight Eisenhower's famous farewell speech, where he described the dangers of 'unwarranted influence, whether sought or unsought, by the military-industrial complex.'*

ORIGINS OF THE DEEP STATE

The idea of a parallel government formed by big business, the military and the government isn't new in American lore. The concept was first articulated in President Dwight Eisenhower's famous farewell speech, where he described the dangers of 'unwarranted influence, whether sought or unsought, by the military-industrial complex.' Such a union between the military and its suppliers would keep the country in perpetual war to enhance its own profits. But this isn't the shadow government that American deep state proponents are referring to when they tout their own theories.

A car crash on 3 November 1996 in Susurluk, Turkey, killed not only a high-ranking police chief but a leader of the right-wing militant group Grey Wolves – and badly injured a member of Turkey's parliament. The question of why these people would be in the same car drove an investigation that revealed the deep connections between Turkey's nominally democratic government, organized crime syndicates and law enforcement – all of whom had united in opposition to Kurdish separatists.

That alliance became known as the 'deep state', a term that was soon applied to a number of countries where a supposedly democratic government is controlled by a nebulous alliance of the military, criminals, industry and the media. Evidence of such states-within-states has been found in a number of Middle Eastern, African and Central American countries; with Egypt being seen as one of the worst offenders.

The deep state isn't just a modern phenomenon, as historical examples of a state that's not technically a military dictatorship but heavily controlled by a military and media apparatus included Imperial Japan, Nazi Germany, the Ottoman Empire and the Soviet Union and its satellites. It often took the form of a heavy-handed secret police that seemed to operate under its own legal precepts, and a military with an almost independent leadership.

THE TRUMPIAN DEEP STATE

The conspiracy theory version of the deep state is not this. America does not have a secret police that arrests scores of the leader's enemies, nor does it have deeply buried alliances between street gangs, local government and the police. What Trump supporters and the conspiracy community call the deep state varies depending on who you're talking to. All believe it to be a cadre of 'permanent power' thugs dedicated only to keeping their grip on the government. But who they are exactly is a bit of a mystery.

Some believe it to be the undue power held by American intelligence and federal law enforcement, working in secret to bury Trump in investigations. Others think of it as an anonymous cadre of lifetime civil servants who slow-walk Trump initiatives and leak to the press. Democrats who have put up constant opposition to Trump are also considered a deep state, as are liberal media outlets, left-leaning businesses in tech and social media, and pretty much anyone else who opposes the president.

The leaks to the media are seen as a particular weapon of the anti-Trump deep state, with anonymous administration sources popping up in countless news articles that have blown open facets of the Trump/

The idea of a 'deep state' was first expressed in President Eisenhower's farewell speech.

Russia scandal. President Trump even blamed 'unelected deep state operatives who defy the voters to push their own secret agendas' for the anonymous editorial in the *New York Times* in 2018, supposedly written by a senior Trump official working to resist the president from the inside.

Trump has pushed back hard against hires he feels aren't loyal enough, and civil servants thought to be trying to undermine him from within. In just a couple of years in office, Trump has already fired more high-level officials in his own administration than any other president, and his staff has fired or banished hundreds of other career employees to bureaucratic purgatory. He's even fired many of the lawyers and officials responsible for the firing of other employees.

The existence of such a deep state is all but canon among Trump and his most fervent supporters. Former Press Secretary Sean Spicer said it's 'no question' that the deep state is working to stop Trump, while Sean Hannity has decried 'deep state crime families' he believes are 'trying to take down the president.' Ex-campaign managers Corey Lewandowski and Steve Bannon both have run with the idea of a deep state made up of both outsiders and traitors within, and a slew of right-wing pundits have written books with titles like *Killing the Deep State* and *The Deep State: The Fall of the Constitution and the Rise of a Shadow Government.*

But one clue to the conspiracy theory nature of the anti-Trump deep state is how difficult it is to define. Whatever the far right thinks the deep state is, it's not what controls countries like Turkey and Egypt. In those nations, a police state operates on a parallel track alongside the actual government – and those who stand in its way suffer far worse fates than being fired.

Beyond that, the deep state is often simply used as a catch-all to describe anyone who opposes Trump. Everyone from billionaire financier George Soros to low-ranking FBI agents to the non-existent paedophile rings at the heart of the 'QAnon' conspiracy theory have been lumped in with the deep state. In most cases, the bigger and harder to define a conspiracy theory, the less likely it is to be true.

Of course, it is quite likely that a number

Former White House Chief Strategist Steve Bannon has decried the existence of a deep state working against Trump's interests.

of career employees in the government are trying to stop Trump. The president entered office with a self-imposed mandate to destroy the 'administrative state' and drain what he called 'the swamp' of unelected bureaucrats. This has manifested in the rollback of laws designed to protect consumers, the environment and the poor. The president has also shown no real interest in giving his own agencies the resources they need, leaving countless major positions unfilled, and budgets slashed.

Why wouldn't these people try to resist the president trying to ruin their professional lives? Likewise, the president has made a sport out of insulting the intelligence community while disregarding their work. It's entirely plausible that some have secretly gone to the media with damaging information, out of a desire to protect national security.

But is this an organized 'deep state' like the ones that plague dictatorships? Or the inevitable result of a government in opposition against itself?

It's clear that the 'state within a state' is a problem that plagues many countries. But the deep state that Trump and his supporters see lurking around every corner is one of both their own making and their own imagination.

The investor George Soros has been identified as one of the members of the deep state by conspiracy theorists.

False Flag Shootings

One of the central concepts of the modern conspiracy movement is that the governments of the world are constantly using faked incidents and terrorist attacks to push their agenda upon the rest of us. So virtually every time a shooting, bombing or car attack takes place somewhere in the world, the term 'false flag' is applied to it – taking a real military term for attacking under a false identity and applying it far past its defined usage.

Conspiracy theory sites are full of lists of 'admitted' false flag attacks, including everything from Nero's burning of Rome and faked Nazi aggression implicating Poland as a pretext for war, to the 11 September attacks and the Boston Marathon bombing. Such long lists of perceived conspiracy theories are usually easily dismissed as fallacious arguments for events that can't be proven. Except for one inconvenient fact: many of these listed incidents are actually false flags, and we know they are. In fact, the use of disguises and trickery as a pretext for military action has been either the real or hypothesized kick-off event for some of the most destructive military conflicts in human history.

A British 'Q-ship' from World War I. Disguised as merchant vessels, 'Q-ships' would lure ships closer before opening fire, in an early example of 'false flag' attacks.

REAL FALSE FLAGS – FROM MUKDEN TO MOSCOW

The term 'false flag' originated with naval warfare, when a ship would run up a flag other than its designated battle ensign in order to draw an enemy ship closer – then run up its real battle flag (fighting while actually pretending to be your enemy being against the rules of war) and open fire, catching the enemy unprepared.

During the World Wars, the allies made extensive use of 'Q-Ships', military ships disguised as unarmed merchant vessels designed to lure enemy ships closer. Another example was the 1942 British raid on the German-held dock at St. Nazaire, France, when the Royal Navy rebuilt an old destroyer to look like a German patrol boat, then sailed it under a German flag to get close enough to the dock to blow it up.

These tactics were also common during land warfare, such as the famous German plan to use English-speaking commandos dressed in American uniforms to carry out sabotage behind Allied lines during the Battle of the Bulge. While most of these men were shot upon capture, the operation itself was later declared to be legal because

the action didn't order them to actually fight while pretending to be Americans.

Japanese troops enter Manchuria after the Mukden Incident in 1931.

False flags also include attacks where soldiers of one country carry out an action against their own people in order to pin it on another country or group they want to go to war with. In fact, it was two false flags that kicked off World War II – both extremely transparent, but just real enough to be useful.

Japan kicked off its 1931 invasion of Manchuria with a staged bombing of the Japanese-owned South Manchuria Railway, using a tiny explosive that was so ineffective that a train went over the railroad minutes later. But this fake attack, later called the 'Mukden Incident', was all the justification Japan needed to invade Manchuria. The German invasion of Poland was also preceded by dozens of incidents involving German troops dressed in Polish uniforms carrying out random acts of vandalism, destruction and terror along the Germany/Poland border. After a slew of these faked attacks, Germany invaded Poland.

Many other famous false flags that led to military conflict have been long suspected as having been carried out by (or at least exploited by) the country that absorbed the attack. The 1898 sinking of the USS *Maine* by what was probably a coal explosion sent the United States to war with Spain over Cuba, while the Reichstag Fire that allowed Adolf Hitler to suspend civil liberties in Nazi Germany has been blamed by a number of historians on the Nazis themselves, despite a Dutch communist being executed for the crime.

In more recent history, the Gulf of Tonkin incident in August 1964, where North Vietnamese patrol boats attacked an American destroyer, is often called a false flag. One attack was real, but a second reported attack several days later was likely only sailors shooting at shadows.

The remains of apartment buildings in Moscow after the September 1999 bombings. These attacks were used as justification to invade Chechnya, even though the police caught an FSB agent in the act.

Nevertheless, President Johnson used the two incidents as a pretext to begin bombing targets in North Vietnam. And the horrifying Moscow apartment bombings in September 1999 that killed over 250 people ensured the election of Vladimir Putin, who quickly cited it to justify invading Chechnya – even after local police arrested FSB agents in the process of setting off one of the bombs.

FALSE FALSE FLAGS

These incidents, real and debated alike, are not the same definition that conspiracy theorists have for 'false flag'. To conspiracy believers, there is virtually no incident of any kind that's not staged by the powers that be to excuse aggressive actions against the population. Almost every American mass shooting of the last two decades has been labelled a government-planned false flag to strip away gun rights. The Sandy Hook shooting, the Pulse Nightclub massacre in Orlando, and the Las Vegas Strip attack in October 2017 were labelled as staged attacks minutes after they happened, fuelled by social media rumours of second shooters and faked victims.

The same holds true for attacks outside the United States. The London bombings of July 2007, Anders Brevik's massacre in Oslo in 2011, the 2015 *Charlie Hebdo* shooting and the Berlin Christmas market attack of 2016 were all deemed by conspiracy theorists to be government-concocted plots, carried out to advance draconian security measures, influence domestic policy or simply to strike terror into the people.

It's understandable why conspiracy theorists look at these incidents and include them with the very real false flags of the past. After all, many *did* lead to draconian security measures and fear in the populace. But does that mean they were faked?

Historical false flag attacks were carried out to meet narrow objectives. For example, the faked Polish aggression against Germany wasn't simply done to advance nebulous ideas of 'consolidating power' or 'taking away rights'. It was to justify a specific course of action against one nation. This is a hallmark of conspiracy theories – they are full of details, but usually in the support of something extremely vague and unclear.

The proof that these incidents were faked usually depends on evidence known to be either fake or taken completely out of context. They mistake a lack of known motivation for a greater sinister intent, particularly with mass shootings, where the killer often takes their own life, leaving behind little in the way of motive or explanation for their actions.

And while some of these incidents have resulted in new laws, most haven't – particularly when it comes to guns. If these shootings were faked by the US government to strip away gun rights, the government has failed every time. Gun access in America is just as easy as ever, and the country hasn't passed major gun legislation since the now-expired Assault Weapons Ban in 1994.

None of these shootings or attacks have ever been proven to have been carried out by that particular government. In most cases, they would involve conspiracies so massive and labour-intensive that they'd fall apart at once. Real false flags have eventually been proven with evidence – or at least involve a theory that's plausible. But the 'staged mass shooting' theory has never had any compelling evidence that's stood up to scrutiny, and few are plausible.

While it might be easier to believe that the rulers of the world send shooters into schools and buildings into planes, that doesn't mean it's true. And a historical event happening once doesn't mean it's happening every time. If everything is a false flag, then nothing is.

Flowers surround the Las Vegas sign in memory of those who died from the 2017 shootings.

Donald Trump, Russia and WikiLeaks

■ It's the question that has dominated political discourse in the United States for years, both leading up to and after the election of Donald Trump: what was the relationship between the Trump Campaign and Russia, and what was the connection between those two entities and WikiLeaks? The myriad of links between the members of Trump's inner circle to moneyed and powerful entities in Russia, and the underbelly of intelligence gathering around the world is a conspiracy so vast that untangling it has been compared to the gigantic spider web of criminality that made up the Watergate scandal of the early 1970s.

Both involved intrigue and possible wrong-doing at the highest levels of power in the United States, and both completely took over the media

Donald Trump shakes hands with Vladimir Putin at a conference in 2018. The links between Trump and Russia have spawned a myriad of conspiracy theories.

landscape of the time. But Watergate is comparable to the Trump/Russia intrigue in another way: much of it lived in the land of conspiracy theory until it was proven to have come true. For the first few months after a gang of burglars was caught breaking into the Democratic National Committee headquarters in the Watergate Hotel, the role of President Nixon and his inner circle remained the subject of countless theories, with little hard evidence. Nixon defenders claimed the president had been set up by the CIA to get him out of office because he favoured detente with the Soviet Union, a theory buoyed by the connections several of the burglars had to the shadowy agency. At the same time, Democrats and liberal writers were seen as overly hyping the severity of the break-in, the conspiracy to cover it up and Nixon's role in it. It wasn't until August 1974, when the 'smoking gun tape' of Nixon ordering interference into the investigation was made public, that Nixon was fully and completely implicated. He resigned a few days later, and what had been conspiracy theory was now simply a conspiracy.

Trump supporters, as well as the president himself, insist that there was no collusion, and that Democrats and liberals working in a 'deep state' are desperate to avenge the loss of the 2016 election. At the same time, anti-Trump politicians and pundits point to his seeming soft stance on Russian president Vladimir Putin, the mysterious inflows and outflows of cash into the Trump Organization, and the already known attempts by Russian intelligence to interfere in the election through hacking Democratic Party organizations and spamming American voters with inflammatory social media. Even the conclusion of Special Counsel Robert Mueller's nearly two-year investigation into the connection between Trump and Russia hasn't quelled conspiracy theories. Trump supporters hailed the letter from the Attorney General claiming the investigation found no collusion between the campaign and Putin,

The Watergate Complex in Washington DC. Until the discovery of the tapes, much of the news of the Watergate Scandal was little more than a conspiracy theory.

while Trump detractors pointed out that the letter specifically did not exonerate the president.

SIGNS THAT IT'S A CONSPIRACY THEORY

Both conservative Trump supporters and liberal Trump resistors have pet conspiracy theories that have inflated to cartoonish versions of themselves. They take real facts and real unanswered questions, and weave them together with fake facts and questions that nobody would even ask, because they're so ridiculous or implausible. At the centre of one allegation is the idea that Donald Trump was elected President of the United States while simultaneously being an asset of the Russian government, who helped Trump steal the election through massive hacking, outright changing of voter rolls and a stack of compromising material on the sexual and financial habits of the Trump inner circle. And that in return for his fraudulent election, Trump is being allowed to consolidate a vast amount of power while giving away America's sovereignty. The end result will be a Trump dynasty passed down through generations with the suspension of elections and rights, all the while controlled by Vladimir Putin and his successors.

Both conservative Trump supporters and liberal Trump resistors have pet conspiracy theories that have inflated to cartoonish versions of themselves.

Simultaneously, to his most slavish devotees, Trump is target number one of a deep state consisting of the CIA, FBI, Justice Department, the entire mass media, the Democratic Party, the National Security Agency, the Federal Reserve and the New World Order. And they conspire together to thwart Trump through relentless leaks to the media, massive donations to the Clinton Foundation, mass brainwashing of Americans through liberal media and manipulating the American economy to make Trump look like he's damaging it. And when that doesn't work, the deep state simply conducts fraudulent elections, getting millions of ineligible illegal immigrants to vote, while colluding with Russia on such hack jobs as the famous 'Steele Dossier'.

If either one of these hypotheses were proved to be true it would signal nothing less than the collapse of the world order we've come to know, usurped by an unaccountable and uncontrollable conspiracy.

SIGNS THAT IT'S A CONSPIRACY

At their worst, these theories become so far-reaching that they collapse under their own weight. Liberal conspiracy theories become shot through with dystopian paranoia, and conservative ones with an almost delusional worship of Trump. The idea that Trump is some kind of Russian sleeper agent benefitting from a stolen election is just as absurd as the idea that every misstep of his administration is due to an octopus of deep state tentacles tripping it up, and that Trump is God's anointed saviour who has done absolutely nothing wrong. Somewhere in these two extremes is the truth.

As of 2019, the Special Counsel has indicted over three dozen people connected to the Trump campaign or in Russia. While there has been no direct link between the hacking, WikiLeaks and the Trump campaign, circumstantial evidence points to a clear connection. Beyond that, Trump's fealty towards Vladimir Putin is inexplicable and obvious, and the financial connections between Trump and Russia are numerous and troubling. Yet conservatives are right that as of now, there hasn't been a smoking gun linking Trump directly to Russia, and we don't know who or what prompted the interference on his behalf. And for all of the accusations of election hacking and voter fraud, neither have proven to be true. There is no giant mass of undocumented immigrants voting Democrat (if there was, they must have sat out 2016), nor is there a massive plot to hack voter rolls and change votes. Not one vote has been found to have been changed. The great autocratic crackdown prophesized by liberals hasn't come to pass, and many of Trump's more inflammatory attempts to assert presidential power have been blocked by the courts. And there have been instances when FBI and CIA employees have been found to be working against the president, but that doesn't make them part of a massive and omnipresent deep state.

The true nature of the connections between Donald Trump and Russia might not be known for years, or even decades. The extremes on both sides, however, are too implausible to be true. It's just not known right now. We know there were crimes and misdeeds and mistakes on both sides of the 2016 election, but their existence is far more likely due to greed and simple human ambition than a massive conspiracy to end the western world as we know it. In the end, like Watergate, everything will be known. And that's the point where we'll know if the conspiracy theories were really conspiracies, or merely theories.

Robert Mueller, the Special Counsel investigating Russian involvement in the 2016 Presidential election, was appointed in May 2017 after the former investigator FBI Director James Comey was dismissed by President Trump.

The CIA and AIDS

Was HIV, the scourge of world health for two decades, secretly invented by the CIA, the scourge of free people since the 1950s? That's what a surprisingly virulent conspiracy theory holds, one that began almost as soon as the Centers for Disease Control (CDC) unveiled the cause of the mysterious 'gay cancer' cutting a swathe through large urban centres. But unlike many of the more outlandish conspiracy theories of the 1980s and 90s, the idea that the US government had a hand in the creation of the AIDS virus is not based merely on unsourced accounts and incomprehensible arguments. There were serious concerns early in the AIDS epidemic that the government was dragging its feet on research and treatment, and that the disease was the most prevalent among the populations that white evangelical America had the most trouble with: homosexuals, drug users and African Americans.

And unlike many other conspiracy theories of the time, this one garnered attention far beyond the US and Western Europe. The conspiracy still has a massive impact on AIDS treatment and prevention in the developing world, sewing distrust in new medications and government-run prevention campaigns. In South Africa, the United States' involvement in AIDS is such a given that nearly a third of gay men in Cape Town believe it. And in the US, a 2005 survey found that nearly 50 per cent of black men think HIV was man-made, and that a cure for the disease was being withheld from the poor so they could be used as medical guinea pigs.

Where do these theories come from? Why would so many people believe that the US government created and unleashed a weapon to cull certain parts of the population, while simultaneously researching new treatments for it?

A TERRIFYING NEW DISEASE REQUIRES NEW EXPLANATIONS

The conspiracy theory that the US created AIDS as a weapon has its origins in something that should be familiar to any follower of contemporary politics: Russian disinformation. And it started in 1983, before the origin of AIDS as caused by HIV had been scientifically confirmed. Seeking to play

A poster issued by the US Centers for Disease Control in 1993 to warn about the dangers of AIDS

If Your Man Is Dabbling In Drugs... He Could Be Dabbling With Your Life.

Shooting up or skin popping, if your man is sharing needles he could get the AIDS virus and bring it home to you. So if he's running with the drug crowd, even if it's only on the weekends, you need to talk to him. Try to get him into counselling. Insist that he wear a condom every time you have sex. And if he's not listening to you —do something to save your life. Leave.

For more information about AIDS, call:
NATIONAL AIDS HOTLINE
1-800-342-AIDS
Servicio en Espanol
1-800-344-7432
TTY-Deaf Access
1-800-243-7889

AMERICA RESPONDS TO AIDS

U.S. DEPARTMENT OF HEALTH AND HUMAN SERVICES
Public Health Service

on the fears of both minority communities in the US and people in the developing world, the KGB began an organized campaign to make people think that the US had invented AIDS to cull those deemed to be undesirables.

It began with an anonymous letter in a pro-Soviet newspaper in India supposedly from an American scientist claiming that AIDS had been bio-engineered in the Army's chemical weapons lab at Fort Detrick, Maryland in 1977 and 1978. More Soviet puppet media figures pushed the story out into African news outlets, and by 1987 it was being covered on the CBS Evening News. By that point, the American conspiracy theory community latched on to it, with alternative medicine practitioner William Campbell Douglass claiming that the World Health Organization invented AIDS to cleanse Africa for colonization in his 1989 book *AIDS: The End of Civilization*. William Cooper's famous 1991 conspiracy tome *Behold a Pale Horse* used misconstrued Congressional testimony to 'prove' that the US had been developing 'a new infective micro organism' since 1969, and blaming it on a coalition of powerful elites and Jews.

The Soviet disinformation campaign was enormously successful. By the mid 1980s it was practically common knowledge among black populations that AIDS was an American biological agent run amok in populations that were denigrated and marginalized under the Reagan administration. And the theory had celebrity adherents. Bill Cosby claimed in 1992 that if AIDS 'wasn't created to get rid of black folks, it sure likes us a lot', while Will Smith speculated that AIDS was 'possibly created as a result of biological-warfare testing.' Nation of Islam leader Louis Farrakhan claimed that new AIDS therapies like AZT were part of the conspiracy as well. African news and politics were full of accusations that the US and/or

Building 470 at Fort Detrick was the location of America's biological weapons research programme.

William Campbell Douglass claimed that the World Health Organization was responsible for creating AIDS.

Yevgeny Primakov, the director of the Russian Foreign Intelligence Service, admitted in 1992 that the Soviets had run a disinformation campaign about AIDS.

A man is x-rayed in the Tuskegee Syphilis Experiment in 1932. The experiment engendered significant distrust among the African-American community.

white South African doctors were smearing condoms with HIV, using it to poison food and pollute rivers, and even testing new forms of the disease disguised as cures – causing a deep vein of suspicion against white doctors, their diseases and their drugs.

REASON TO BE SUSPICIOUS

While these seem like implausible plots full of assumed details, there are good reasons to be suspicious of the American government's role in medical research. In 1932, the Public Health Service began a six-month experiment on African American men in rural Alabama to study syphilis. But it misled its subjects into giving informed consent, and faked their treatments, lasting decades after a cure for syphilis was widely available. The lies went on for 40 years. At the same time, the CIA was experimenting with hallucinogenic drugs and mind control as part of the MKULTRA project, often on unwitting subjects. Thanks to a harsh media spotlight and outrage from Congress, both of these illegal human experiments became public knowledge in the mid 1970s, only a few years before the first Soviet conspiracies about AIDS.

It's not surprising that the African American community embraced these conspiracy theories. AIDS was first confirmed in 1981, but it took until 1985 for Ronald Reagan to acknowledge its existence, in a press conference where he hinted that children born with HIV shouldn't be allowed to stay in school with non-infected children. At the height of the conspiracy, the mid to late 1990s, the government had long shifted its stance on AIDS, and treatments for HIV were available – but were expensive and hard to get. And AIDS still was far more prevalent in marginalized communities than in the white middle class mainstream. Even after a decade, African Americans represented nearly 50 per cent of new HIV cases diagnosed in the United States, far outstripping their demographic percentage.

AN IMPOSSIBLE TIMELINE

The conspiracy theory is falsified by the very nature of how AIDS works. The trajectory of a disease

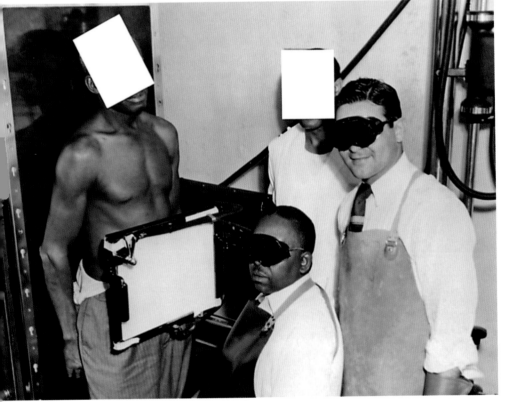

that takes between 10 to 15 years to manifest simply doesn't match up with the conspiracy theory that the US created it in 1977. By 1981, when the CDC identified that AIDS had become an epidemic, it had been in the US population for a decade. We now have a fairly well established chain of events for how it originated, starting with cross-species transmission of the simian immunodeficiency virus from primates to humans, possibly as early as the 1920s. The first deaths from what later became identified as AIDS took place in the early 1960s in Africa, and it entered New York in the early 1970s, mistaken for virulent pneumonia. The epidemic was in full bloom when the conspiracy says it began. Beyond that, if AIDS was meant to purge gay men and drug users, it failed. There are now treatments for HIV that render it a chronic illness, rather than a fatal disease – though it still requires a daily regimen of multiple expensive medications to control.

And if the CIA did indeed invent AIDS, it didn't bother protecting its own agents very well. According to declassified documents, it wasn't until 1987 that the agency began alerting personnel in high-risk countries about the potential for contracting HIV from sexual encounters, and it didn't start testing prospective employees until later that year. By that point, the AIDS epidemic was already in full swing, likely claiming the lives of CIA agents as well as the population it was supposedly created to wipe out. Ultimately, the CIA creating AIDS is a plausible conspiracy theory not because of its mechanics, but because of the people involved – and that's not, in and of itself, proof of a conspiracy.

Ronald Reagan is handed a report of the presidential commission on AIDS by James D. Watkins. Reagan did not acknowledge the existence of the disease until 1985, four years after it had been identified as an epidemic.

Agenda 21 and the UN

■ Conspiracy theories about the United Nations have existed since the first meetings of the international body. Radical far-right elements like the John Birch Society have spent decades calling the organization a prelude to one-world government, a front for communism, a vehicle for the return of the Antichrist, an unholy alliance with some meddling foreign power (usually Jews), an earth-worshipping hippie cult, and a front for global genocide through vaccines.

These conspiracy theories, almost entirely propagated by American and European conservatives, see the UN as a bloated and useless bureaucracy bent on sucking up more power and controlling our food, water, air, politics, transportation and religion. In the end, its controllers will eradicate those deemed by them to be 'useless eaters' and plunder what's left for themselves.

Speculated plots about world government are not new, of course. They didn't even start with the UN. When the League of Nations was formed out of the ashes of World War I, isolationist Senator Henry Cabot Lodge gave a thunderous speech calling it a 'mongrel banner' and declared that if the United States became entangled in the affairs of Europe, it would 'destroy her power for good and endanger her very existence.'

But while these and subsequent conspiracy theories have drifted in and out of favour as the decades have gone on, the most prevalent one of the last decade has a firmly 21st century origin. In fact, it revolves around humanity's transition into a new century, and even includes its name – Agenda 21.

A PLAN TO RADICALLY CHANGE HUMANITY?

Agenda 21 is a non-binding, unenforceable policy paper, developed in 1992 and signed by 178 countries, including the United States. Declaring that 'human beings... are entitled to a healthy and productive life in

The United Nations are at the centre of the conspiracy theory regarding Agenda 21.

harmony with nature,' Agenda 21 is a long-term plan for environmentally-healthy development, more efficient use of land and resources, improved urban planning, promoting wellness, combating poverty and reducing our impact on the land and water.

Among its objectives are promoting international trade that takes account of the needs of developing countries, better data collection and research, enabling the poor to achieve sustainable livelihoods, encouraging greater efficiency in the use of energy and resources, meeting primary healthcare needs, and reducing health risks from environmental pollution and hazards.

Agenda 21 has no penalties for non-compliance, no enforcement arm to ensure any element is carried out and no requirements for how it's implemented. You can put into practice some, all, or none of it. Most of it is carried out at the community level, and it's meant to be most impactful on local issues such as traffic and resource use, with no oversight from the United Nations. And the plan is available online in its entirety, in a variety of languages. The world signed on to Agenda 21, and began implementing these sound and evidenced policies.

But two decades later, it became an Obama-era lightning rod for conservatives already feeling the heat of liberal fascism breathing down their necks. A wide range of Republican governmental bodies, pundits, writers and voters see Agenda 21 as nothing less than a nightmarish vision of the future, a horror show of draconian regulations and population transfer where environmental impact will be put before human happiness. And that's just for the lucky ones who aren't eliminated – a figure that some conspiracy videos peg at 95 per cent of the population. In the end, the planet will be a barely populated playground for the elite,

At the Earth Summit in Rio de Janeiro, 1992, the UN met to discuss environmental issues. The outcome of the summit was the signing of Agenda 21, a plan for sustainable, environmentally-friendly development.

with the survivors turned into little more than slaves of the UN, worked to death to support the elite.

But even a cursory reading of Agenda 21 shows none of that. So why is there such a disconnect between the real Agenda 21 and the conspiracy theory version?

WHICH IS THE REAL AGENDA?

Despite Agenda 21 having been signed in the early 1990s, it had almost no real footprint in the conspiracy theory world until late 2011. That was the beginning of an almost unceasing drumbeat of paranoia from conservative media figure Glenn Beck, who spent hours on multiple media platforms declaring that Agenda 21 was a diabolical plan to destroy local communities and 'centralize control over all of human life on planet earth.'

Beck even wrote a 2012 book called *Agenda 21*, (or rather, he put his name on a book written by someone else and grabbed the bulk of the royalties) where America has been replaced by a fascist state called 'The Republic'. In the Republic, there is 'no president. No Congress. No Supreme Court. No freedom,' as the book's promotional blurb puts it. 'There are only the Authorities. Citizens have two primary goals in the new Republic: to create clean energy and to create new human life.

Glenn Beck, a conservative talk show host, decried Agenda 21 as a plan to establish control over everyone on the planet.

Those who cannot do either are of no use to society.' The original book was described by its editor as an enjoyable dystopian novel, something akin to *The Handmaid's Tale.* But Beck's involvement sent it rocketing through the ranks of the conservative movement as a document to be taken seriously.

The Republican National Committee put language in the official 2012 election platform decrying Agenda 21 as a 'comprehensive plan of extreme environmentalism, social engineering and global political control.' Multiple state legislatures passed laws banning any kind of involvement with it. And local tea party groups began protesting at planning commission seminars, city council hearings, zoning

boards and board of supervisors meetings.

The impact of these protests was far from just symbolic. In 2012, voters in Georgia voted down a one-cent sales tax meant to shore up crumbling Atlanta roads, largely due to fear of it being tied to Agenda 21. Multiple other states scuttled plans for bike lanes and high-speed rail tracks, and major cities were prevented from tracking carbon emissions and electricity usage. During his successful Senate campaign, Texas' Ted Cruz ran on opposing Agenda 21 as a plan to 'abolish...golf courses, grazing pastures, and paved roads.'

Conspiracy theorists on social media even shared an 'Agenda 21 death map', supposedly showing all the areas in the US where the population would be culled.

Ted Cruz based his 2016 Presidential campaign on opposition to Agenda 21.

IS ANY OF THIS HAPPENING?

Agenda 21 was passed in 1992 – and yet not a single UN apartment block has appeared, no populations have been culled and nobody's golf course has been confiscated. Virtually none of the nefarious bike lane and carbon tax plans that have been linked to it actually are related to it, and the hysteria mostly died down after the 2012 election. Many communities have quietly and readily put its recommendations into practice, with notable improvements in carbon emissions and traffic. The plan has gone through a number of iterations and alterations, and a follow-up plan called '2030 Agenda for Sustainable Development' was passed by 193 UN member states in 2015.

Of course, conspiracy theorists attached themselves to that plan as well, calling it 'global socialism' built around population control, curtailing of free travel and trade and the 'removal' of the Second Amendment. But the new version didn't catch fire the way Agenda 21 did, at least not at the local level. Opponents seemed to realize that if the UN actually had a plan to purge the population, they'd manage to get around to it at some point.

If the world is going to withstand climate change, it will require extensive adaptability and flexibility about resource use. Agenda 21 and its successors are a path towards that – and it's understandable that many will resist any sort of change brought about by the UN. Even if that change is positive.

COVER-UPS

What happens when the string-pullers need to make sure the rest of us don't find out about something terrible they did? They cover it up! And yet, they do it so badly and sloppily that we find out about it anyway, usually with just a bit of internet searching. From crashed planes that were 'really' hit by missiles to the goings-on at Area 51 to the real shape of the earth, here are the conspiracy theories about what the powers that be have been keeping from you.

The Malaysian Airlines aircraft that mysteriously disappeared on 8 March 2014.

The Disappearance of MH370

Major aviation disasters tend to spawn conspiracy theories because of their scale and rarity. In fact, there was not a single death from a passenger jet crash in 2017, and just 271 in 2016. So when a large passenger plane crashes or disappears, it inevitably becomes fodder for conspiracy theories because we believe it's one of those things that isn't 'supposed to happen'.

And no passenger plane disappearance has spawned more conspiracy theories than Malaysia Airlines flight MH370, a Boeing 777 with 239 passengers and crew that disappeared on 8 March 2014. Air traffic control lost contact with the plane an hour after it left Kuala Lumpur, and after a series of unplanned turns and sustained silence, the plane's footprint was reduced to a series of automated satellite pings, then a faint echo on military radar – then nothing.

The aircraft 9M-MRO disappeared on a Malaysian Airlines flight from Kuala Lumpur to Beijing in 2014.

The plane's ragged flight path, and the vast stretches of ocean it flew over, meant that rescuers had no real idea where to look. But a massive effort saw over two dozen nations contributing to a hugely expensive

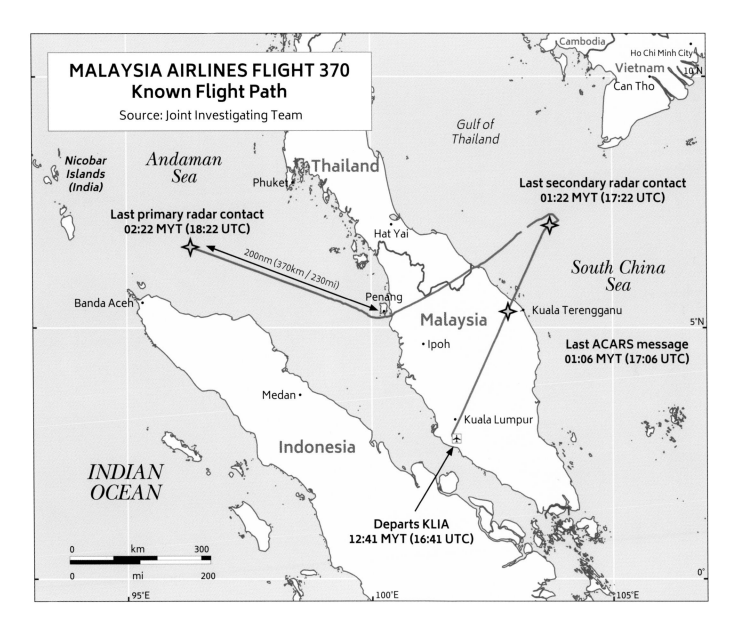

MALAYSIA AIRLINES FLIGHT 370
Known Flight Path
Source: Joint Investigating Team

Cambodia
Ho Chi Minh City
Vietnam 10°N
Can Tho

Gulf of Thailand

Nicobar Islands (India)

Andaman Sea

Thailand
Phuket

Last secondary radar contact
01:22 MYT (17:22 UTC)

Last primary radar contact
02:22 MYT (18:22 UTC)

Hat Yai

South China Sea

200nm (370km / 230mi)

Banda Aceh

Penang

Malaysia

Kuala Terengganu

5°N

Last ACARS message
01:06 MYT (17:06 UTC)

Ipoh

Medan

INDIAN OCEAN

Indonesia

Kuala Lumpur

Departs KLIA
12:41 MYT (16:41 UTC)

| 0 | km | 300 |
| 0 | mi | 200 |

0°

95°E   100°E   105°E

operation that resulted in nothing recovered. The first debris washed up on a beach in July 2015 on Reunion Island in the Western Indian Ocean, not even close to where the plane's flight path took it.

The gap of time between the plane's disappearance and the first debris appearing was filled to the brim with conspiracy theories, allegations, plots and fantastical guesses about what happened.

The flight path of MH370 shows its departure and the locations of the last contact made with the plane before its disappearance.

PLANES DON'T JUST DISAPPEAR

In the hours after MH370's disappearance, there was little available information that wasn't maddeningly vague. So in the absence of evidence otherwise, conspiracy theories caught on with people looking for a way to explain something that seemed to have no explanation – which was pretty much everyone. They proceeded over several parallel tracks. The first was that the plane was hijacked, and either flown somewhere or crashed. The second was that it was shot down. The third was that a crew member committed suicide by crashing the plane. The

The US military installation on the island of Diego Garcia in the Indian Ocean. Some have speculated that the plane was captured by the Americans and taken there.

fourth was that the plane suffered a devastating accident that Malaysian Airlines was desperate to cover up. All the theories worked under the same assumption: that aeroplanes don't simply vanish. Something had to happen to them.

The hijacking theory had some appeal after the plane's initial disappearance. MH370 was last sighted on military radar over the Andaman Sea, west of Thailand and north of Indonesia. A study by an aviation expert found as many as 600 runways in that area where the plane could have landed, and there were two Iranian passengers found to have had stolen passports. But the point of hijacking an aeroplane is to ransom it for money or something else, not crash it or disappear. Still, theories persisted that involved the plane being hijacked by 'jihadis' (put forth by Rupert Murdoch, no less), hijacked via remotely activated malware, grabbed by North Korea, or captured by the US and taken to the military installation Diego Garcia. The Malaysian government's own report, released in July 2018, doesn't rule out 'unlawful interference by a third party' in the disappearance of the plane, but offers no proof of it either.

The second conspiracy track, that the plane was shot down, got a big boost when a book appeared just two months after the crash alleging that the plane was accidentally downed by either the US or Thailand during a joint exercise. It would certainly be the easiest way to explain what happened to the plane. Even Rush Limbaugh got in on the act, spinning an un-evidenced theory that the plane suffered a 'total electronic failure' and was then shot down by a 'hostile country' who quickly figured out and buried their mistake. Such accidental shoot-downs have happened before, including the downing of an Iranian Airlines flight by a US cruiser in 1988, and the Soviet shoot-down of Korean Airlines Flight 007 in 1983. But these incidents quickly became public, and were impossible to bury. Beyond that, a plane that crashed because of a missile hit leaves an enormous amount of closely-distributed debris. That's clearly not the case for MH370.

The third theory, that one of the pilots steered the plane into the ocean, isn't unheard of, with flights in 1997, 1999 and later in 2015 all going down due to pilots committing suicide. And the theory gained some credence when it was revealed that the pilot had recently split up with his wife, flown the plane off course to go past his home island of Penang, and had no social plans for after 8 March. But the pilots were scrutinized, and neither were found to have either mental health issues or involvement with terrorism. Beyond that, the pilot having no plans for after the flight turned out to be a rumour, as he had a dental appointment scheduled for later in March. Even so, the 2018 Malaysian government

An SU-15 interceptor, the type of plane that shot down Korean Airlines Flight 007 in 1983.

Don Lemon, a CNN host, proposed one of the wilder theories about what happened to MH370 when he suggested it had fallen into a microscopic black hole.

report noted it was a 'plausible' theory.

After that, the conspiracy theories start to get wilder. One got traction when CNN figure Don Lemon rhetorically asked 'is it preposterous?' about MH370 being swallowed by a microscopic black hole. Another saw a complicated (and debunked) conspiracy to eliminate the holders of a patent on a new type of semi-conductor. Other experts speculated that the plane landed in the jungles of Cambodia full of bullet holes, thanks to a Google maps artefact. Finally, a CNN poll found that nearly 10 per cent of respondents found it 'plausible' that the plane was taken by time travellers, aliens or inter-dimensional beings.

A LONG, SILENT DEATH FLIGHT

The fourth conspiracy theory track, an accident (probably an electrical fire), seems like the most plausible. MH370 left Kuala Lumpur and continued northeast for an hour. Civilian radar lost contact with it over the South China Sea, but military radar tracked it as it changed direction and headed southwest. It flew back over Malaysia and then changed direction again, heading northwest. That's where it vanished for good. At that point, the automated communications system had been damaged, hence the inability to contact or track the plane. And through all that flying, no emergency locator was ever activated.

The changes in direction and lack of communication are consistent with the pilots diverting course, desperate to find somewhere to land. But if they flew over Malaysia, why not land somewhere there? We don't know, of course. The plane made multiple turns, and overflew several potential landing sites.

The most plausible explanation is that they were incapacitated, due to carbon monoxide from a fire. By that point, the plane would be a flying graveyard, with everyone on board dead from lack of oxygen or suffocation and nobody to land it. It would run on autopilot, full of corpses, until it ran out of fuel – either gliding into the water at low speed and sinking, or spiralling down into a high speed dive that hit the water so hard the plane simply disintegrated into pieces too small to be found.

But what caused the fire? Why didn't the pilots land over Malaysia? Why so many turns? Why not activate the emergency locator beacon? We still don't know, and might never know. And that's the one conclusion that's the hardest to accept – never knowing what really happened.

In January 2017, the search for MH370 was suspended for good. The final report by Malaysian authorities, released in July 2018, was over 1,500 pages – and none of them contained a final answer as to what happened, just plausible theories and theories that were less plausible. But debris is still being found to this day, including a piece of plane found off the coast of Madagascar in January 2019. Will any of it lead back to the plane, and more importantly, an answer to what brought it down? The most plausible answer is that we don't know.

Australian ships search for evidence of the debris from MH370 in April 2014.

Area 51 and UFO Disclosure

No government facility has as much of an imprint in conspiracy culture as the one commonly known as Area 51. A mysterious, sprawling compound in the foreboding flats of the Nevada desert, Area 51 is where some of America's most advanced aircraft have supposedly been tested.

Those who work there can't discuss what they do, and those who try to get in are greeted with threats that they will be shot on sight. Beyond that, some conspiracy theorists believe it to be a place where alien ships are back-engineered, powerful weapons developed and aliens themselves tested on. If it wasn't, they reason, why is there so much mystery surrounding the place? Why don't we know anything about what's happening now and what's been done there in the past? And why, to this day, are alien-looking craft spotted flying there?

But while Area 51 was indeed once shrouded in mystery, recent intelligence disclosures have taken much of the intrigue away from the place. Area 51, which is never actually called that by the people who work there, is still a classified test facility doing things that the general public will likely never find out about. But thanks to declassification and former employees being allowed to tell their stories, we know a great deal about the place's past – and how the work done there has changed aviation history.

SECRET WEAPONS AT A SECRET PLACE

Warning signs surround the Air Force facility in Nevada, providing fuel for the conspiracy theorists' fire.

Like so many other subjects, conspiracy theories about Area 51 caught on because it's a real place – surrounded by real secrecy. While the Air Force generally doesn't acknowledge its existence, the fact that it does exist has been common knowledge for three decades. Yet everything that happens there is classified at the highest level – Top Secret/Sensitive Compartmented Information.

This puts Area 51 into a hazy area: a real place that spends tax dollars on projects that tax payers aren't allowed to know anything about. This secrecy wasn't always baked into the facility, however. In its earliest incarnation, the dry bed at Groom Lake, Nevada, was

Groom Lake in the Nevada Desert is the location of Area 51, an American government facility shrouded in mystery.

simply a pair of unpaved runways used during World War II, and given the un-mysterious name Indian Springs Air Force Auxiliary Field.

In the early 1950s, the Atomic Energy Commission was looking for places to set off nuclear bomb tests, so they bought up a huge tract of desert, called it the Nevada Test Site, and parcelled it into numbered Areas. A few years later, the CIA needed a place to test a high-flying spy plane codenamed AQUATONE. The flat land of Groom Lake was perfect, and so an unused part of the Nevada Test Site was designated as Area 51, and became the location where AQUATONE was put through its paces.

Over the next few decades, the tract of land expanded to include about 1,000 employees – many flown in from Las Vegas or Los Angeles on secretive, unmarked flights. AQUATONE gave way to an even faster reconnaissance plane known as OXCART, and Area 51 also became the destination of choice to test captured Soviet fighter planes, as well as testing of two alien-looking stealth planes known as HAVE BLUE and TACIT BLUE.

None of this was public at the time, of course. In fact, Area 51 had no real public imprint until 1989, when a man going only by the name 'Dennis' told a Las Vegas TV reporter a fantastical tale of alien ships, fantastical-looking craft and secrets of the highest nature. 'Dennis' claimed to be an engineer at a classified testing facility called S-4, located near Area 51. 'Dennis' worked in a hangar built into a mountainside, back-engineering a disc-shaped alien spacecraft to reveal its secrets: anti-gravity propulsion, the ability to change directions on a dime, invisibility and incredible power driven by an undiscovered element. 'Dennis' learned about earth's involvement in a 10,000-year pact with a civilization from the Zeta Reticuli star system, and about forms of physics and engineering that were centuries ahead of our own technology. He claimed to have taken part in test flights of nine different alien craft, and been involved in the explosion of an alien element.

The Lockheed A-12 reconnaissance plane, developed under the codename OXCART, had a distinctly alien look to it.

A photo of the military base at Area 51 taken in 1996.

Within a few years, the conspiracy theory about Area 51 had grown to encompass the cold storage of alien bodies taken from the Roswell crash, faked moon landings, mutated Soviet midget pilots, weather control mechanisms, directed energy weapons, and tunnels to secret underground bases which were all alleged elements of the 'real story' of Area 51.

And these stories were augmented by countless UFO sightings of strangely shaped aircraft doing strange things in the sky over Area 51, not to mention the unmarked planes carrying employees and the total silence from anyone in the government about all of it. The CIA even forbade NASA from publishing an image taken via satellite of the Groom Lake area in 1974 – an event revealed in a memo declassified in 2006 that called Groom Lake 'the most sensitive spot' on earth.

The goings-on at Area 51 are just one part of a supposed 'secret space programme', theorized by conspiracy believers as a parallel NASA, using alien and back-engineered Nazi technology to build giant bases on the moon, anti-gravity spacecraft, powerful energy weapons, and even study the rudiments of time travel and light speed.

And it's still happening. In February 2018, two amateur UFO spotters made national news when they captured footage of two F-16 fighters appearing to dogfight a triangular craft jumping around in the sky. Naturally, the Air Force had no comment.

THE SECRECY FALLS AWAY

Much of what happens at Area 51 is still classified, but the bloom of secrecy has decidedly gone off the facility. The government made its first declassification of Area 51 documents in 1991. That's when longtime UFO watchers were mildly disappointed to learn that AQUATONE was actually the U-2 spy plane, OXCART was the codename for the SR-71 spy plane, and HAVE BLUE was an early concept version of the F-117 stealth fighter. This oddly-shaped plane fits perfectly with the description of the craft seen flitting about the Nevada skies.

In 2007, many former Area 51 employees had their confidentiality agreements lifted. Cold War-era workers who'd been silent for nearly 50 years told incredible stories of working on deeply classified projects,

being paid in cash or by non-existent front companies, scaring off local deputies who arrived at sites where secret planes crashed, and, oddly enough, how great the food was. They were proud of the work they'd done, and reunions of former Area 51 employees were common – though always secret. And there was even more disclosure of classified information in 2013, when the CIA officially acknowledged its existence thanks to a Freedom of Information lawsuit. What none of these reports contained were long-held secrets about aliens, anti-gravity, faked moon landings, or UFOs. There weren't any. 'Dennis', who first put the idea of aliens at Area 51 in popular culture, turned out to be a UFO enthusiast named Bob Lazar who never attended any of the advanced schools he claimed to have, and likely spent very little time at Groom Lake – yet still clings to his stories of fantastical technology and alien experimentation.

What really happens there now is still classified, of course. Radio traffic there is still coded to mask the names and types of planes flying in and out, and snoopers who find ways to evade security will likely learn little and quickly be sent away. But while the secrecy is still there, the idea of Groom Lake being 'the most sensitive spot on earth' is falling away. Google Maps includes outlines of the airstrips at Groom Lake, the 'triangular craft' seen dogfighting F-16s in 2018 was quickly revealed to be a bird, and the Air Force is even posting job ads for pilots to ferry staff from Las Vegas' McCarron Airport to the base. But the planes they'd be flying are still unmarked.

The HAVE BLUE project was a prototype for the F-117 stealth plane. This plane was a good match for the descriptions of UFOs seen over Nevada.

A map of the Nevada test range around Groom Lake, where Area 51 is located. The veil of secrecy around the area is slowly being lifted, and now even Google Maps shows the airstrips at the base.

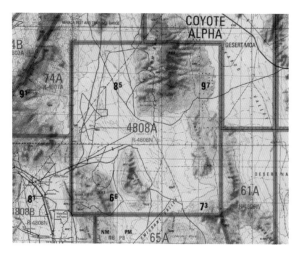

The Crash of TWA Flight 800

Late in the evening on 17 July 1996, TWA Flight 800 took off from New York's John F. Kennedy Airport on a transatlantic flight to Paris. But just 12 minutes into the journey, the plane suffered an explosion, and crashed into the Atlantic Ocean off the coast of Long Island. There were 230 passengers and crew on board, and none survived.

The sheer loss of life and the rarity of major aviation accidents in the United States, along with the nascent internet conspiracy theory movement, combined to create what was maybe the first large-scale online conspiracy theory related to a plane crash. Such theories are almost a foregone conclusion now, with virtually every major air disaster run through a grinder of false flag allegations, wild theories and connections between minor events. But in 1996, culture in general, and fringe culture in particular, moved much slower. So when a plane full of people simply disappeared, and was the subject of a massive investigation, it naturally led to allegations that the government was lying about what really happened.

The possibility that the plane was shot down by the government, either accidentally or on purpose, became so hotly debated that the government itself carried out tests to disprove it. But did they?

A DOOMED FLIGHT, AN INSTANT CONSPIRACY

The location of the crash caused the National Transportation Safety Board's investigation to take much longer than a normal plane crash might. To the NTSB's credit, they managed to recover all of the 230 bodies in ten months, and reassemble 95 per cent of the plane's frame, with the missing pieces deemed too small to be of significance.

But even as debris was painstakingly being moved from the ocean floor to a hangar in upstate New York, a parallel narrative was building: that witnesses saw an 'ascending streak of light' moving towards a part of the sky where a large fireball appeared. The FBI interviewed over 750 witnesses, and over 250 described variations on the same thing: a bright object spiralling, ascending, or streaking

The reconstructed wreckage of the plane from TWA Flight 800. Almost the entire plane was recovered.

towards an aeroplane, followed by an explosion, with the sound following closely behind, and the target falling into the ocean in two pieces. In fact, 38 described such a streak ascending vertically, almost straight up – exactly like a missile would.

The FBI then contracted the CIA to use summaries of this eyewitness testimony (the interviews weren't recorded) to create an animation of what the witnesses described. And that testimony and animation, along with the involvement of America's most shadowy intelligence agencies and the slow pace of the NTSB investigation, led observers to come to one conclusion: Flight 800 was shot down by a missile.

These theories burbled for years, until the NTSB released its final report in August 2000. The government agency found that Flight 800 was split in two by the explosion of flammable fuel vapours in the plane's centre fuel tank, probably caused by a short circuit in faulty wiring. The explosion sent the two large pieces descending into the ocean, where both shattered.

While the centre fuel tank explosion theory was plausible, the NTSB paid heed to the conspiracy theories. They ran a variety of tests on what witnesses would have seen if a missile had shot the plane down, and deduced that the eyewitness testimony was mistaken. They even tested what it would look like if a missile exploded near the plane, as well as testing what a bomb explosion would do to the plane's frame.

But while the missile theory was disregarded by the report, it resulted in two more nagging questions: why did the plane have 196 tiny impact points on its frame? And why were there trace amounts of explosive residue detected on three samples of material from the recovered aeroplane wreckage? Such impacts and residue would be consistent with the shrapnel caused by a missile exploding next to the plane. And wouldn't the NTSB, an arm of the government,

An eyewitness to the explosion answers questions about what happened. Many witnesses described an 'ascending streak of light', implying that a missile had been fired.

Two members of the NTSB take out the voice recorder and flight data recorder from TWA Flight 800. These revealed a normal take-off but failed to reveal the cause of the explosion.

have the motive to cover up the destruction of a passenger plane? If the government shot the plane down accidentally, it would be a scandal of epic proportions. And if it was brought down by terrorism, it would mean every passenger plane in the world was vulnerable to the forces of evil – possibly bringing down the entire airline industry.

CONSPIRACY THEORIES CAN'T CHANGE THE LAWS OF PHYSICS

So who fired the missile? Why? And how did it happen? Such a missile would have to have been fired from something, either another aeroplane, a land-based instillation, or a boat. Was there anything in the area that could have launched it?

The US military reported that the only aircraft in the area of Flight 800 were a P-3 Orion anti-submarine plane, an HC-130P air-sea rescue support plane and an HH-60G rescue helicopter. While an Orion can theoretically carry air-to-air missiles, they would have no particular reason to be armed with such weapons during peacetime. The other craft don't have the capability to shoot another plane down. The only American naval vessel within eight hours of the area was the Coast Guard Cutter USS *Adak*, armed with only small calibre guns. The *Adak*'s crew won the Coast Guard Unit Commendation for their search and rescue work in the aftermath. If the *Adak* had shot down the plane (with weapons it doesn't carry), would it return to the scene of the crime? After that, there was only the cruiser USS *Normandy*, located almost 300 kilometres south of where Flight 800 exploded – far out of range of anti-aircraft missiles.

A P-3 Orion anti-submarine plane was the only aircraft in the area of the doomed flight. It is unlikely that it would have been carrying air-to-air missiles.

Without resorting to making up 'stealth' assets or secret weapons, the next possibility for a missile would be a land-based installation, but there are none in the area of the crash armed with surface-to-air missiles. And while some conspiracy theories have pointed to either a shoulder-fired or submarine-fired missile, no man-portable anti-aircraft missile has anywhere near the range needed to have shot down Flight 800. And submarine-launched anti-aircraft missiles have never been deployed in the US Navy due to their inaccuracy.

Any other unknown asset would need to have been scrubbed from the records of every military and civilian radar in the area, with everyone

The USS Adak responded quickly to the disaster and played a major role in the search and rescue efforts, but that has not stopped conspiracy theorists from suspecting the vessel of foul play.

able to report on such an asset eliminated. It would also require all evidence of a fired missile being eliminated, and the faking of a four-year NTSB investigation. Hundreds or even thousands of people would need to be involved, multiple murders would have to be carried out and reams of evidence would have to be destroyed. It would be a cover-up of massive proportions.

Paradoxically, it would also have left seemingly hundreds of witnesses, whose testimony was eventually released publicly. It affirmed that what most saw was consistent with two large, flaming pieces of an aeroplane streaking towards the water. Other testimonies claim to have simultaneously seen and heard the streak and explosion – violating the laws of physics, as the light of the explosion would have been visible about a minute before the sound drew the ears of the witnesses.

As for the minor impact holes? They were likely caused by debris hitting the plane after the explosion. And the explosive residue probably wasn't on the plane initially, as contact with the water would have diluted it. Instead, it was likely the result of the boots of military personnel contacting the wreckage.

In 1996, the internet was ripe for an anti-government conspiracy theory taking off. Flight 800 was the perfect mix of unusual events, government involvement and tragedy. But nothing in the intervening years has changed the NTSB's findings: an internal explosion caused by fuel fumes sparking. It was a once in a decade tragedy, with no satisfactory explanation other than bad luck.

Flat Earth

After persisting as a fringe movement for decades, the belief that earth is actually flat, and not a globe, and that the entire scientific establishment is lying to all of us, suddenly experienced a massive spike in popularity in early 2015.

What drove this surge isn't clear. It's certainly not anything that could be construed as a new scientific discovery – since the scientific community has known for 2,500 years that the world is round. It's far more likely that it's a combination of social media, general distrust in institutions and the decline of critical thinking in western society that's caused a not-small number of people to think the earth is flat.

And yet, they do. The new 'flat earth' movement has drawn tens of thousands of people into various Facebook groups, spawned countless popular YouTube videos and debates, caught the eye of minor celebrities and even forced popular science communicators to respond to it.

Surveys back up this disturbing trend. A February 2018 survey from

A flat earth map drawn by Orlando Ferguson in 1893. It shows the Antarctic as a wall of ice surrounding the edge of the world.

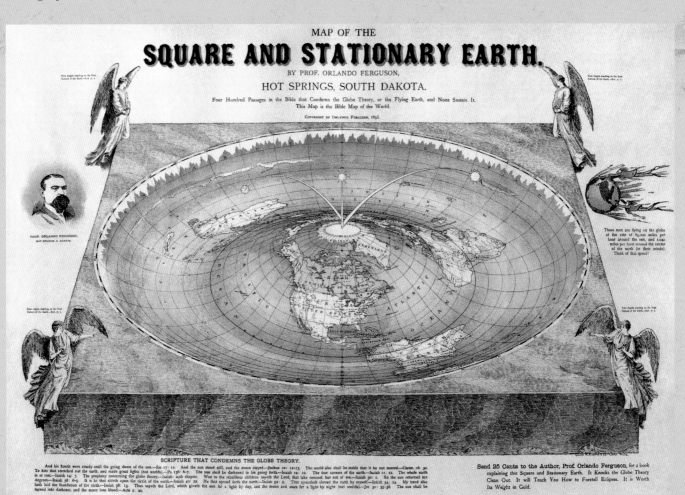

YouGov asked 8,200 Americans if they 'believe that the world is round or flat', and only 84 per cent answered that they had never believed the earth wasn't round. It also showed that 2 per cent of Americans believe with no doubt that the earth is flat, and as many as one-third of those age 18 to 24 either harbour some doubt that the earth is round, or weren't sure either way.

The evidence for it depends on scientific concepts that are either wilfully misunderstood or simply made up. When cornered, many flat earthers fall back on insults, generic arguments to 'do your own research', or change the subject.

But is there any evidence? Or is the flat earth movement merely one designed to de-centralize knowledge and put very basic scientific concepts (such as what the earth looks like) into the hands of the people who recently had knowledge handed down to them from on high?

WHAT DOES A FLAT EARTH LOOK LIKE?

Contrary to popular misconception, neither ancient people nor those living afterwards believed the earth was flat. While many ancient societies did depict the planet as flat and surrounded by water, by the 5th century BC, the Greeks had carried out rudimentary experiments proving that the earth was a globe, though they didn't know how big it was.

The great Pythagoras was involved in some of the earliest efforts to prove the earth was round. Likewise, Aristotle noted that various signs of a spherical earth, such as how ships disappear over the horizon and the position of stars moving, 'show not only that the earth is circular in shape, but also that it is a sphere of no great size: for otherwise the effect of so slight a change of place would not be so quickly apparent.'

Nor did Christopher Columbus go 'sailing the ocean blue' to prove that the earth was round. That bit of lore came from a story by Washington Irving. And Galileo wasn't sent to his death for disputing the Catholic Church's belief in a flat earth, as Thomas Jefferson wrongly wrote a century earlier.

Flat earth mythos was mostly the stuff of arguments between various religious factions until the late 1800s, when a book called *Zetetic Astronomy: The Earth not a Globe* articulated the claim that the planet was a flat disc surrounded by ice walls – with hell itself lying beyond those icy cliffs. That book, written by Samuel Rowbotham under the pseudonym 'Parallax',

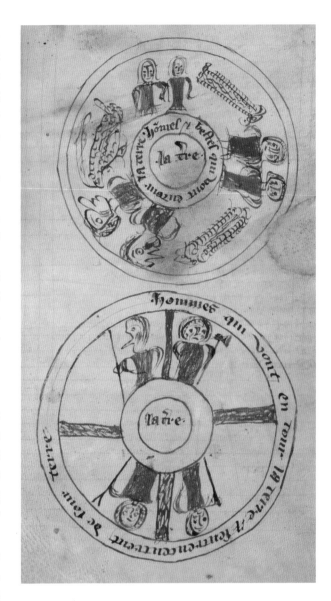

Contrary to popular belief, in the Middle Ages most people believed the earth to be round. This image from a 14th-century manuscript depicts a spherical earth.

The front cover of Zetetic Astronomy, written by the flat earth campaigner Samuel Rowbotham, who went by the pseudonym Parallax.

Samuel Shenton founded the International Flat Earth Research Society in 1956.

took off in certain English circles and spawned a debating society and several well-known attempts by believers to prove the flatness of the earth. Eventually, the Zetetic movement became more about opposition to established science in general, and it died out after World War I.

But its basic tenets were picked up by an English sign painter in the 1950s, who founded the International Flat Earth Research Society based on the Zetetic movement – though not sharing much of its actual beliefs. That group eventually turned into a purely non-scientific Christian fundamentalist conspiracy mongering group, and then into an online only forum dedicated to conspiracy theories, which now has about 11,000 members and doesn't talk much about flat earth.

WHAT DO FLAT EARTHERS BELIEVE?

The basics of flat earth belief vary, but generally, you're likely to find most believers think the earth is some kind of flat disc, and that the scientific establishment has lied to us about what our senses 'really' tell us.

Many flat earth debates become entangled in minute aspects of science and weather that most people don't understand. The depth and detail of these discussions ends up lending credence to what they discuss, as if any scientific theory that wasn't true simply couldn't have as much sheer material to debate. Part of this debate revolves around the misuse of scientific jargon, deploying concepts like 'crepuscular rays' (sunbeams shining through clouds) proving that the sun must be much closer to the earth, and gyroscopic attitude indicators on planes staying horizontal during flights. These are real things, but are totally misinterpreted by flat earth believers.

To explain away the vast amount of pictures of the earth as a globe, they just claim every photo of a 'globular' earth was either distorted by a fisheye lens, or faked. They also throw out things that are true, but have perfectly reasonable explanations, such as there being no direct flights across the South Pole from Chile to New Zealand, that large bodies of water don't wobble due to spinning, or that it's impossible to see the curve of the earth at the height commercial airlines are allowed to fly at. Indeed, long lists of such 'proofs' of flat earth are the lingua franca of the movement, demanding enormous time and effort to debunk – hence few people doing it.

Beyond that, the bigger a flat disc is, the more distorted the gravity becomes away from its centre, which is why galaxies are flat with spiral arms. On a flat earth, weather and daytime would function totally differently, because of distorted gravity. Many flat earthers claim that gravity itself

The flat earth conference in Denver, November 2018. The flat earth movement has grown rapidly in popularity since 2015.

is also a hoax, and the flat earth is accelerating upwards, propelled by 'universal acceleration'. This is not a concept that has ever been proven to be possible. But it's central to flat earth, and is the only thing that would explain why the sun rises and sets over a flat earth, or why the stars change their positions.

Some flat earthers seem to understand how little evidence there is in favour of their argument, and are less interested in trying to thrash out the intricacies of things like why the earth would be the only flat planet in the solar system, and are more interested in simply questioning everything around them. Indeed, flat earth beliefs are almost entirely intertwined with conspiracy theory beliefs as a whole, which is consistent with established research showing that if you believe one conspiracy theory, you're likely to believe others. Believers spend as much of their online time talking about 'waking up' and 'doing research' in general as they do about flat earth in particular. They distrust scientific authorities, governments and popular figures who tell us to assume the earth is round. They put their faith in their senses, their biases and what they want to be true, rather than what others tell them. And there's a nasty strain of anti-Semitism in the flat earth movement, like there is in almost every moderately popular conspiracy theory.

In the end, any time spent in the flat earth community reveals that it's hard to tell who truly believes it, who's just there for laughs and who will believe any conspiracy theory put in front of them as long as it implicates 'the powers that be'.

Nibiru/Planet X

■ Stories of great space cataclysms are a staple of both literature and science. Some of it is good old fashioned folklore, passed down through the generations. And some is scientifically accurate work that's been studied for decades, such as the generally accepted theory that a massive asteroid impact in the Yucatan caused the mass extinction that wiped out the dinosaurs. But there are also a number of people who have seized on the alluring idea of a hidden planet or asteroid lurking out there in the darkness to advance their own conspiracy theories, sell books, or set themselves up as modern day prophets.

The 'Nibiru' conspiracy theory falls squarely into that last category. Every few years, tabloid articles and pseudoscientific prophecies seem to hail the coming of a planet-sized object in a distant orbit that will impact earth at a time only they know for sure – a time that never seems to arrive. While Nibiru, the name often given to that object, is a different concept from that of 'Planet X', the two are often lumped together and used as interchangeable terms. One is an actual scientific theory that

An artist's impression of the possible ninth planet in the solar system, with the orbit of Neptune around the sun shown in the distance. The search for 'Planet X' has occupied the minds of both the most accomplished astronomers and the most fervent conspiracy theorists.

has been proposed by great minds in astronomy, and meticulously studied over the span of decades. The other is a fantastical concept of a woman who claimed to have been experimented upon by aliens, working from a book written by a supposed scientist and linguist who actually had no background in either. Determining the differences between the two is a useful way to practice scientific scepticism, as well as to introduce critical thinking concepts into a story that often gets hyped far beyond its importance.

THE STORY OF NIBIRU

The idea of a large, undiscovered planet lurking beyond eighth planet Neptune has fascinated astronomers for over a century. In fact, even before Neptune was discovered in 1846, scientists believed a massive object must be responsible for the irregularities in the orbit of seventh planet Uranus. They saw deviations in its trajectory that seemingly only could have been caused by the gravity of something extremely large and close. In 1906, American astronomer Percival Lowell began searching the skies for an object he called 'Planet X', with the X signifying 'unknown' rather than the number ten, as Pluto hadn't been discovered. Lowell's search, along with the investigation of a number of other astronomers, proved fruitless, even after Pluto was found, as the former planet wasn't big enough to be the source of Uranus' anomalous orbit. No other trans-Neptunian object was ever found that would fit the description needed.

The astronomer Percival Lowell (1855–1916) began searching for the mysterious 'Planet X' in 1906.

It's very common for pseudoscience to attempt to explain something that science can't. So it shouldn't be surprising that a series of cranks, fake prophets, and others rushed into the void left by the non-discovery of Planet X. In the mid-1970's, when it was becoming clear that Pluto wasn't the large object past Neptune that had been hoped for, an author and pseudohistorical scholar named Zecharia Sitchin made up his own explanation. His 1976 book *The 12th Planet* posited a massive planetoid depicted in Sumerian mythology as the cause of a number of mass extinctions on Earth, and gave it the name 'Nibiru' based on his own translation of an unknown word found on a cuneiform tablet. At no point has any reputable scientist or astronomer confirmed that Sitchin's Nibiru is real, and if it actually did exist, it would be so disruptive to the orbits

The conspiracy theorist Nancy Lieder argued that the Hale-Bopp comet, which passed by earth in 1995, was being used as a distraction from the real danger of the 12th planet.

of the actual planets that the solar system would essentially fly apart. It would also be easily seen in the night's sky. Beyond that, Sitchin's grasp of the Sumerian language was rudimentary, and it's likely that he mistranslated the tablet he was working with.

But none of those objections made any difference to Sitchin's growing fanbase, who readily bought a seemingly endless series of books about the secret goings-on in history and astronomy. One of Sitchin's most vocal fans was a woman named Nancy Lieder, a self-described psychic and telepath, claimed to have been kidnapped and experimented upon as a child by aliens from Zeta Reticuli (also the home of David Icke's world-dominating 'reptoid' aliens (see pages 47–8.) Lieder had started the website ZetaTalk in 1995, as an early hub of discussion about aliens, UFOs, and conspiracy theories. Around that time, as the Hale-Bopp comet was approaching its closest distance to Earth, Lieder put forth a shocking theory on ZetaTalk: that Hale-Bopp was actually being used as a diversion from the real threat to Earth, which was the 12th planet, making its once-every-3400-years approach.

'Hale-Bopp is nothing more than a distant star, and will draw no closer,' Lieder wrote on the site on 6 August 1995. 'The 12th Planet, a true messenger of death, will not even get the attention the fraudulent Hale-Bopp is getting today. That's because it's a real threat, not a diversion.' This was the first of dozens of posts she made about the 'Hale-Bopp Fraud' she felt was being pulled on us by NASA and the scientific establishment, who would do anything to keep the people from learning the truth for fear of panic. The theory caught on with the conspiracy theory media of the time, making Lieder a radio star, and raising her profile to the point that when she declared that Nibiru would hit the Earth around May 15, 2003, it made mainstream news.

2003 – OR 2012 – OR 2017

The day 15 May 2003 came and went without the cataclysm Nancy Lieder had spent almost a decade predicting. Rather than abandon the 'Nibiru' conspiracy theory, she doubled down, saying the date she'd thrown out was merely a bit of disinformation 'designed to fool the establishment'. She then claimed that only she knew the real end-of-days date (thanks to the Zetans who continued to communicate with her), and that giving out the real date would only allow the establishment to keep citizens from fleeing to safety. As with most other conspiracy gurus, Lieder gave out a torrent of implausible and unverifiable claims to bolster her writing, giving it the appearance of profundity.

Regardless, Nibiru was sucked into the frenzy of conspiracy theories and mythology surrounding the Mayan calendar/2012 phenomenon. Despite Mayan and Sumerian mythology being completely different, Nibiru fit well into the hazy beliefs of people who thought the world was ending simply because people they trusted told them so (and the establishment didn't). Again, continuing what conspiracy theorists thought was a massive cover-up, NASA and the science establishment swore up and down that Nibiru wasn't real, and that there was no actual Mayan prophecy about anything happening on 21 December 2012. And they were right, as the 2012 phenomenon was a bust as well. It came back again in 2017, when a fringe astrologer and 'prophet' named David Meade threw out 23 September 2017 as the date that the Bible and an alignment of stars foretold of Nibiru crossing Earth's path. It didn't, so Meade threw out more dates in 2017, then again for 23 April 2018. They all came and went. Meanwhile, evidence that Nibiru or Sitchin's '12th planet' exist continues to be elusive, kept from us not by a conspiracy but by basic science.

We still don't know the source of the gravitational irregularities in Uranus' orbit, though they likely are caused by a long-ago impact pushing the planet onto its side and having its axis point almost directly at the Sun. And scientists continue to scan the skies for objects either past Neptune, or whose orbits take them close to Earth. But the constant drumbeat of prophecies and conspiracies regarding a massive planet that only a few rogue scholars know about has nothing to do with this real scientific research – and everything to do with making money out of the scientifically illiterate.

Conspiracy Theorists merged beliefs about Nibiru with the supposed predictions of the Mayan calendar that the world would end on 21 December 2012.

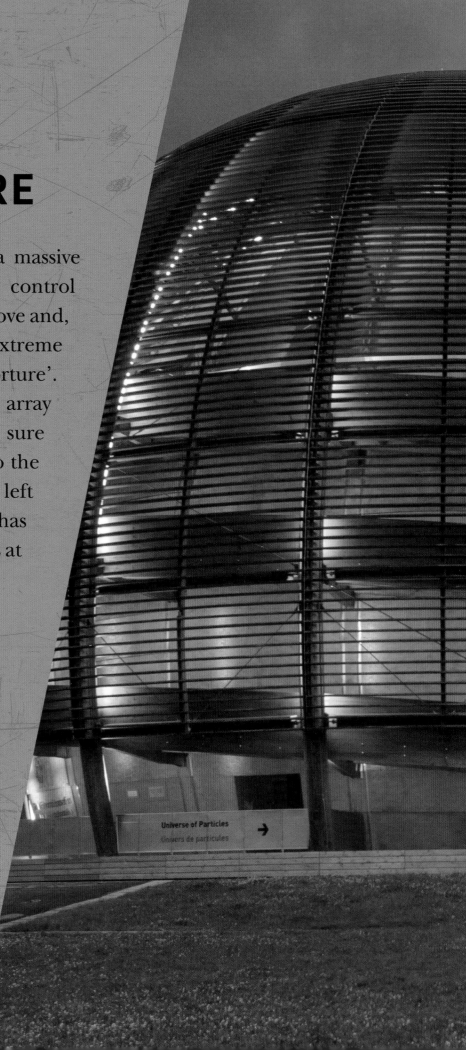

THEY'RE EVERYWHERE

Conspiracy theorists believe a massive array of technology exists to control our minds, spy on our every move and, if needed, punish us with extreme weather and 'touchless torture'. From the mysterious HAARP array in Alaska to the RFID chips sure to be implanted in all of us, to the strange white lines in the sky left by aeroplanes, the deep state has its eyes on us and its claws in us at all times. Or does it?

The CERN research centre in Switzerland, where the Large Hadron Collider is located. To some it represents the pinnacle of scientific research. To others, it is the home of a sinister conspiracy.

HAARP and ELF Waves

■ Located in rural Alaska is a government-created transmitter array that conspiracy theorists believe has the power to harness Extremely Low Frequency (ELF) waves to manipulate the weather, alter the electromagnetic makeup of the atmosphere and even to control minds and cause pain. Its name: HAARP, or High Frequency Active Auroral Research Program.

Since its construction in 1993 by the US Air Force, HAARP has been used to study plasma physics, electron emissions, how atmospheric disturbances affect GPS signals and to observe meteors and solar flares. Because it takes an enormous amount of power to generate ELF waves, HAARP uses a bit of a shortcut, turning the ionosphere into a giant ELF transmitter by hitting it with focused high frequency radio waves. Those waves can then be directed towards either land, the upper atmosphere or the ocean, depending on the subject of the experiment being carried out. In particular, HAARP studies have helped determine how the ionosphere affects communication between submarines and satellites, as ELF waves move more easily through water than air.

The HAARP antenna grid in rural Alaska. The facility sends ELF waves into the ionosphere to discover more about the atmosphere.

But to conspiracy theorists, HAARP is nothing less than a machine that imbues the powers that be with a mind-boggling array of ways to control us and punish those who step out of line. And it's not just conspiracy cranks who think this way. A number of prominent researchers have expressed reservations about HAARP's power, including the brother of a former US Senator, several renowned physicists and military officers and former Minnesota governor Jesse Ventura. ELF waves have been blamed for the rampage at the Washington Navy Yard, where a shooter who claimed to hear voices in his head killed 12 people, as well as physical pain, projections of UFOs and targeted childhood cancers. Could this be possible? Since HAARP is very real, we know a great deal about what it does. But much of this work is complex, esoteric and done in a remote part of the country. Hence, the conspiracy theories trying to figure out what it 'really' does.

ANGELS DON'T PLAY THIS HAARP

The conspiracy theories about HAARP took off thanks to a combination of timing and the people involved with building it. HAARP began operations in 1993, and it took a few more years for the first conspiracy theories about what it 'really' does to hit the media. In 1995, Nick Begich, Jr., the son of an Alaskan congressman, published a book called *Angels Don't Play this HAARP: Advances in Tesla Technology*, making a series of wild accusations. Begich claimed that the array can 'disrupt human mental processes, jam all global communications systems, change weather patterns over large areas, interfere with wildlife migration patterns, negatively affect your health, [and] unnaturally impact the earth's upper atmosphere.' Begich goes on and on describing how HAARP will be used to 'boil the upper atmosphere', 'alter mental functions' and even fry the nervous systems of America's enemies, creating what Begich refers to as 'war without death'.

The book took off in the nascent internet conspiracy movement and among listeners to Art Bell's popular conspiracy radio show *Coast to Coast AM*, and Begich sold over a hundred thousand copies. There is

The governor of Minnesota from 1999 to 2003 Jesse Ventura was concerned that the site was being used by the government for mind control or weather manipulation. His request to visit the facility was denied.

Mobile phone towers are supposedly used to transmit ELF waves across the country.

now conspiracy media all over the internet accusing HAARP of controlling our weather and creating massive superstorms, including strengthening Hurricane Sandy to help Barack Obama get re-elected; of causing and targeting earthquakes against nations that run afoul of the United States; of sending ELF waves bouncing off mobile phone towers for the purposes of tracking our calls and movements; of causing California's recent spate of fires and drought; and even of targeting individual people for harassment through physical and mental pain.

It's also spiralled out into parallel conspiracy theories. One of the most cited is that HAARP was actually developed to harvest natural gas and superheat it into a focused, high-energy beam that could vaporize everything from incoming missiles to enemy cities. Another is that the Russian military believed that HAARP could 'trigger a cascade of electrons that could flip earth's magnetic poles.' It's also linked to chemtrails, UFOs, the coming of the Antichrist and a variety of mostly psychosomatic diseases.

A RESEARCH STATION THAT WASN'T EVEN RESEARCHING

So is any of this true? HAARP has so many claims made about it and against it that debunking them all would involve a book as long as *Angels Don't Play This HAARP*. Begich claims that the array is an extension of the incredibly advanced research that Nikola Tesla did near the end of his life, on topics like electronic power transmission, free energy and horrific weapons like death rays and scalar bubbles – work confiscated by the FBI, never to be made public. It's true that much of Tesla's final work was examined by the FBI (by a physicist uncle of Donald Trump, no less), but that work was found to be mostly delusional self-promotion. Tesla was penniless and likely battling advanced mental illness when he died – and none of the fantastical research he supposedly pioneered in those final days was ever tested or even completed.

Beyond invoking Tesla, a good clue that a conspiracy theory is just a conspiracy theory is that it involves numerous different people making numerous different accusations about the same thing. They can't all be true, and if they can't all be true, why would one be true and another not true? A machine that could control weather *and* fault lines *and* human brains *and* storms would be a scientific marvel on a par with the wheel or fire. But HAARP doesn't have the capability to do any of that, and despite accusations about it being developed by various nefarious actors (usually pegged as the ARCO oil company or the US government's weapons research arm DARPA), it's far less powerful than conspiracy theories would suggest.

HAARP is composed of an observatory and an 11-hectare field with 180 high frequency antennae, each one 22 metres tall, and with 3,600 kilowatts of transmission power. Essentially, these are more powerful mobile phone towers. They can send low frequency radio signals, create a weak aurora that's barely visible at night and slightly heat up parts of the upper atmosphere. ELF waves are useful for passing information through seawater or around the earth, but at such a low data transmission rate that they're useless for anything other than basic communication. They have no ability to do the fantastical things conspiracy theorists ascribe to them, and while exposure to ELF waves has been found to create slight irritation in test subjects, the power needed to do anything more than make someone close by itch would be enormous and impractical.

There's also the matter of HAARP having been closed from 2013 to 2015 due to a lack of funding, after the Air Force decided it wasn't getting its money's worth. And yet, superstorms, earthquakes and headaches all kept happening while HAARP was closed. Fortunately, the University of Alaska Fairbanks acquired HAARP from the Air Force in 2015, reopening it as a scientific research facility open to scientists from around the world, and conducting dozens of experiments each year. And some even use ELF waves.

But even with all that context, HAARP has become a conspiracy theorist catch-all, something they can easily blame for whatever they feel like needs to be blamed on something. The truth is far less interesting – but more accurate.

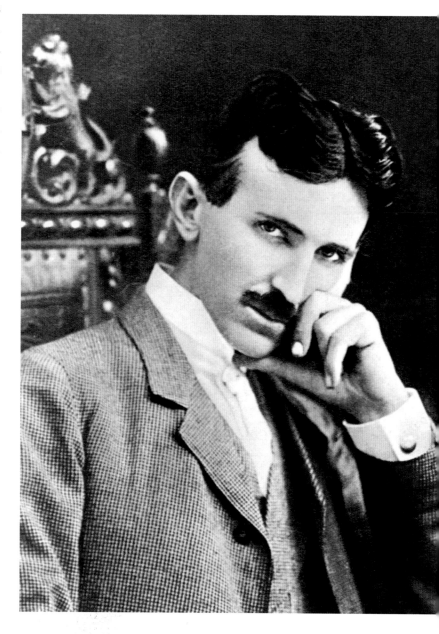

Conspiracy theorists believe that the work at HAARP is a development of the research done by Nikola Tesla toward the end of his life.

RFID Chips

Are they a measure of convenience or an instrument of control? A handy means of tracking valuable items or a nefarious method of surveilling humans? These are the questions that surround Radio Frequency Identification (RFID) chips, small data storage devices that are activated by the radio waves of the device used to track them. About the size of a grain of rice, RFID chips have existed since the early 1970s, and are used for everything from automatic toll collection to supply chain management and tracking livestock to passport control.

Because of their passive energy use, they don't need their own power source, such as a battery. This allows them to be made cheaply, sold in bulk and disposed of easily. And they fit neatly into all sorts of tags, cards and labels. But it's exactly their use for tracking and cataloguing that has put RFID chips at the centre of a nefarious conspiracy theory, one that taps into our deepest fears about surveillance and identity: mandatory RFID chipping of humans for the purposes of tracking, and maybe even herding. After all, if they can track cows and packages, why not humans? Some Christian fundamentalists even see the mandatory insertion of RFID chips as a 21st century version of the biblical 'mark of the beast', a conspiracy theory previously reserved for barcodes.

Putting aside all of the conspiracies, there are real concerns about the safety and privacy of RFID chips, sparking an entire industry of 'RFID-blockers' that will supposedly foil thieves from secretly scanning the chips in your credit cards or pulling your passport information without your consent. And of course, anything that can be used to track people can also be manipulated into spying on them and collecting data. So are RFID chips really a sinister way for the powers that be to track and control our movements? Or just a technology with a lot of uses that we should probably spend less time worrying about?

THE MARK OF THE BEAST

It's almost impossible to separate RFID chip conspiracy theories from their biblical connotations – that their mandatory implanting fulfils the mark of the beast written of in the Revelation of John, heralding the end of the

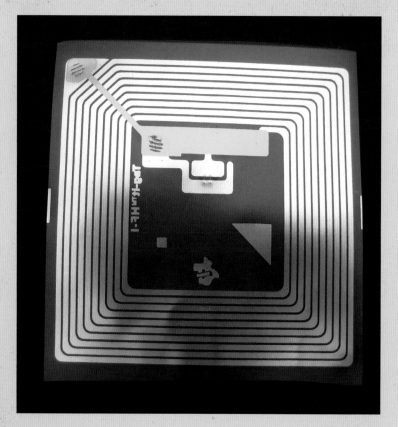

An RFID tag. These tags are activated by radio waves and don't require a power source.

world. Citing the need for Christians to 'consider the industry plans' of RFID use, including 'tracking people around stores, following their movements in public and even spying on them in their homes', the authors of the 2006 book *The Spychips Threat* call on followers of Christ to reject this technology as invasive and ungodly. At the same time, many Orthodox Jews reject RFID technology as a form of 'numbering', which is forbidden in the Old Testament. There are even comparisons by both Jews and Christians to Nazi-era tattooing and marking of Jews, with *The Spychips Threat* authors rhetorically asking 'What if Hitler had RFID?'

The fear behind mandatory chip implantation doesn't just have religious connotations. Privacy experts and libertarians have long argued that at some point, humans will be commonly implanted with RFID chips, giving everyone from our employers to the government the ability to track us. Several American companies already use fitness trackers to log employee physical activity, and a number of state-owned factories and power plants in China use specially designed software to track the brainwaves of their workers. The increased use of 'emotion monitoring' technology led *Business Insider* to call brainwave tracking 'a new stage in China's surveillance state.' Is it any wonder that conspiracy theorists see such danger in RFID tracking? A number of conspiracy theories claimed that the United States' massive healthcare overhaul Obamacare would lead to anyone seeking government-run healthcare to be RFID chipped. Indeed, a deeply-buried provision of the law required that a 'device be implanted in the majority of people who opt to become covered by the public healthcare option', though it only applied to the Department of Health and Human Services creating a registry to track the use of

Orthodox Jews reject RFID tags because it represents 'numbering', which is forbidden in the Torah.

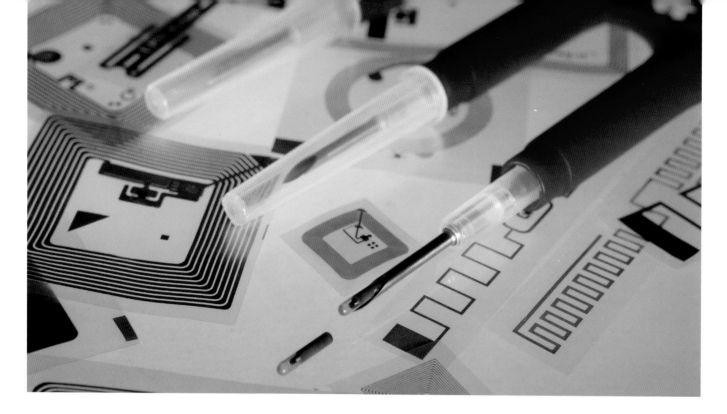

Many believed that Obamacare would introduce the mandatory implantation of RFID chips in anyone who received government-run healthcare.

medical devices. Nonetheless, such rumours about mandatory chipping to facilitate a liberal healthcare law flew during the Clinton and Obama administrations alike.

Finally, there are the sad stories of those who see themselves as 'targeted individuals', innocent people attacked with powerful and secret electronic weapons as test subjects in non-consensual experiments, carried out to test the capabilities of their latest gadgets. TI's, as they call themselves, believe they have been randomly singled out for 'touchless torture', a kind of remote cruelty encompassing everything from electronic harassment to intense physical pain and mind control. And it's coordinated through secretly implanted RFID chips, placed by the government without their consent to help target their torture. While uncommon, this is a real phenomenon, with real victims. Websites catering to TI's are full of tips for how to find and disable the RFID chips they've been violated with, theoretically making it harder for the government to target them – yet even that usually doesn't stop the torture.

OLD CONCERNS MADE NEW AGAIN

Like many new and suddenly omnipresent technologies, it's hard to separate the actual concerns about the safety and security of RFID chips from the supposed horrors of mandatory tracking and touchless torture. Before the idea of mandatory RFID chips spurred 'mark of the beast' comparisons, Christian millennialists were complaining that we'd all be the subject of mandatory barcodes tattooed on our bodies so that the forces of evil could track and herd us. And before that, Social Security numbers were seen as the US government attaching us with the mark of the beast. In fact, there are stories of fundamentalist Christians going to court after being terminated from jobs for refusing to provide their Social Security number – with legal penalties attached to employers who don't report them.

The stories behind 'targeted individuals', while based on real suffering, fundamentally misunderstand how RFID technology works, as the reader must be extremely close to the chip to activate it. While the pain and fear these people express are very real, none of it has ever been proven to have originated from a secret government weapon. Generally speaking, a set of vague and ever-changing maladies with no clear cause or evidence are signs not of electronic attack, but of a psychosomatic illness that can be treated with talk therapy and medication. And much of the 'contactless' payment technology utilizing RFID chips proved unwieldy or unpopular, and was supplanted by payment apps and QR codes. RFID chips are standard on US passports, but they have weak signal capabilities that can only be activated at close range, and RFID credit cards never took off, with the vast majority of credit cards using EMV technology that can only be run through specific readers. But the paranoia is real enough that a number of states have passed laws against theoretical mandatory chipping, while others have banned RFID skimming technology, despite no evidence that any financial crimes have ever been committed through surreptitious scanning of RFID chips.

RFID tracking has legitimate uses, including making sure children get on and off school buses, ensuring the safety of memory-addled residents at nursing homes and replacing fraud-prone employee timeclock technology. Meanwhile, products to block or disrupt RFID signals are big business, despite their having no real use or proof of efficacy. It's frightening to think of the government mandating that we be tagged with tracking devices, but it's clear that such an idea is a flight of paranoia, and not a necessary solution to any real problem.

A Greek nun protests against RFID chips. Christian millennialists see the RFID chips as the 'mark of the beast'.

The Montauk Project

On a remote tip of Long Island, New York, in the hamlet of Montauk, stands either a relic of World War II fears, or an ultra-sophisticated scientific base devoted to some of the most terrifying research in American history. The place is ostensibly called Camp Hero, and is now a state park. But according to an almost limitless series of books, TV documentaries and websites, the US government used Camp Hero to research time travel, the opening of other-worldly portals, the enhancement of latent psychic abilities and psychological warfare. All of this went on for decades, until a few courageous whistleblowers published a book in the early 1990s blowing the lid off the whole evil thing.

What's called 'the Montauk Project' took off just as the conspiracy theory community was making the leap on to the internet. It encompasses a wide range of supposedly secret technology being harnessed by an evil government for sinister purposes, and equally little evidence to support their existence. And these secrets, paradoxically, are reported on so extensively that they are almost common knowledge now. But the

The decommissioned radar station at Camp Hero in Montauk, New York.

Montauk Project is also so compelling to mainstream audiences that it's spawned the hit TV series *Stranger Things*, multiple reality TV shows and countless books. There must be something to the strange doings at Camp Hero that fires the public imagination, even if the more outlandish claims are shrouded in mystery.

Or maybe that's just what they want us to think.

THE HORRORS OF CAMP HERO

Montauk, New York, has a population of just 3,300 people. But its location makes it one of the most strategically important places on the East Coast. The early American military built the Montauk Lighthouse to keep watch for British ships trying to enter Long Island Sound, while during World War II, the Navy turned Montauk into a 112 hectare base full of coastal artillery, docks and planes. That base was named Camp Hero, after a recently deceased Army Chief of Coast Artillery, and would serve as one of the first points of contact should the Axis try to invade New York. The invasion never came, and in keeping with changing technology, Camp Hero was converted into a state-of-the-art radar installation meant to pick up incoming Soviet bombers and missiles. But by 1984, even that threat had largely passed, and Camp Hero was shut down and donated to the state for future use as a park and ecological reserve.

The closure of a fairly sophisticated military facility sparked conspiracy theories that were eventually collected in the 1992 book *The Montauk Project: Experiments in Time*, written by Preston Nichols and Peter Moon. The authors allege, based on Nichols' repressed memories being recovered, that Camp Hero was home to a top-secret experiment. Called the Phoenix Project, it continued work that the US government first began in the 1940s with the 'Philadelphia Experiment', a plot to make a naval warship invisible, only to have it drive its crew to mental breakdown. Funded by Nazi gold, the Phoenix Project built a massive bunker under the camp, and used it to test mind control technology by subjecting kidnapped orphans to massive hits of electromagnetic radiation from a thought-transforming device they called the 'Montauk Chair'. At the same time, the government used secret technology developed by Nikola Tesla to break down the barriers between time and space, once even making a quantum interlock with the original Philadelphia Experiment and bringing two sailors forward in time over 40 years. There were also rumours of alien ships, teleportation, involvement by the Nazi 'Order of the Black Sun', the building of a '50-foot titanium ziggurat' on the grounds, and young boys reprogrammed

Funded by Nazi gold, the Phoenix Project built a massive bunker under the camp, and used it to test mind control technology by subjecting kidnapped orphans to massive hits of electromagnetic radiation from a thought-transforming device they called the 'Montauk Chair'.

The Phoenix Project at Camp Hero was allegedly funded by Nazi gold and was apparently a US military research programme to develop mind control technology.

into super soldiers to be unleashed at the right time. Finally, when the time portal created at Montauk began disgorging terrifying creatures from other dimensions, Nichols could stand no more. He smashed the 'Montauk Chair' and many of the most arcane and horrible experiments ended. No more kidnapped orphans, no more time portals.

Or did they end? In 2008, the carcass of a bizarre creature washed on to the shore of Montauk, a beast quickly dubbed the 'Montauk Monster' by the media, and deemed proof that whatever the Montauk Chair brought through the portal was real – and maybe still around.

STRANGER THINGS – BUT NOT THAT STRANGE

Despite its scattershot approach and lack of evidence, the Montauk Project conspiracy theory took off. After all, the government was already involved in terrible experiments involving mind control and drugs, under the MKULTRA umbrella. And the Cold War was a desperate time where the threat of nuclear annihilation pushed the US to develop weapons once seen only in science fiction. So why couldn't this be true, too? Buoyed by its initial success in the conspiracy community, Nichols and Moon churned out an endless series of Montauk books and allegations, including a sequel two years later, and other books about the 'pyramids of Montauk', the 'Nazi-Tibetan' connection to Montauk and links to aliens from the Pleiades Cluster. Other writers soon took their work and spun it into even more bizarre directions.

As the years went on, the Montauk Project got bigger, more expansive and less plausible. Its 'time tunnel' was said to have changed the outcome of the Civil War, it was supposedly the birthplace of the Men in Black, the headquarters of the 'black helicopters' used by the government against citizens, and where the legendary Jersey Devil monster was spawned. Others accused it of being where the moon landing hoax was filmed, and even where AIDS was invented. Nikola Tesla was alleged to be running the experiments there, despite having been dead for decades, using a staff entirely of Nazi scientists. The conspiracy theories became so expansive that there was simply no credible way for one place to have spawned all of its evil deeds, particularly a place as small and isolated as Camp Hero. It strains even the logic of conspiracy theories that one place could be the site of a 'time tunnel', mind control experiments, psychic chambers and biological laboratories. One, maybe. But all of them?

The authors of the original Montauk Project book never let go of their claims, with Nichols asserting the Montauk story until his death in 2018. And finding a rich vein of fringe material, Hollywood came calling, giving even more credibility to Nichols and Moon. Elements of *Men in Black* and *The X-Files* were based on Montauk mythology, and *Stranger Things* not only used huge parts of the psychic child soldier/ dimensional portal mythos, but was even called 'Montauk' early in its development. But none of it has ever been proven to be real. Camp Hero is now a park and wildlife refuge that gets hundreds of thousands of visitors – and not one has found any evidence of anything the Montauk Project authors allege. Likewise, the Philadelphia Experiment that supposedly formed the basis for the Montauk Project has never been proven to have taken place, while the Montauk Monster of 2008 was almost certainly a decayed raccoon.

Montauk speaks to our desire to see the dark hand of government control in every strange happening, even if they didn't actually happen. But it's also a window into our need for great stories full of bizarre events, heroic whistleblowers, larger than life danger and evil villains in lab coats who come for our children. Montauk has them all. The Montauk Project might remain a myth, but it's powered by some of the oldest notions in the human psyche. And that's why it retains its power.

The Jersey Devil is one of many strange occurrences that has since been attributed to the Montauk project.

Chemtrails

■ The 'chemtrails' conspiracy theory is one of the most mainstream and widely believed on the internet. Its believers think that the governments of the world are using commercial aircraft to spray long paths of unknown chemical substances in the air for a wide variety of purposes, speculating on everything from weather warfare to population control. They claim that the proof is right above our heads. Just look up on a sunny day, and you're likely to see a jet plane with a white line behind it. Some of the clouds dissipate easily, while others seem to hang in the air for long periods of time, with little rhyme or reason.

The technical term for these long aerial paths is 'contrails' – a contraction of 'condensation' and 'trails' that simply denotes the path of ice crystals left behind when hot exhaust from a jet engine hits the cold air of the atmosphere. In fact, there is no evidence that this is not what chemtrails actually are, and an enormous amount of evidence that proves contrails are what we think they are.

And yet, the chemtrails conspiracy theory has reached the mainstream. Multiple YouTube videos offering 'proof' of their existence have over one million views, while dozens of books and thousands of articles have been written about their supposed evils. If one simply looks at the sky, it's easy enough to see the long trails, crisscrossing and smearing all over what would normally be beautiful blue sky and wonder what's really going on.

So what is really going on?

A CONSPIRACY FOR THE INTERNET AGE

One reason it has become so embedded in modern conspiracy culture is that it took off at the same time as the internet itself: the mid 1990s.

A 1996 report entitled 'Weather as a Force Multiplier:

Contrails are the path of ice crystals left behind by the exhaust from a jet engine. These form the basis for the chemtrails conspiracy theory.

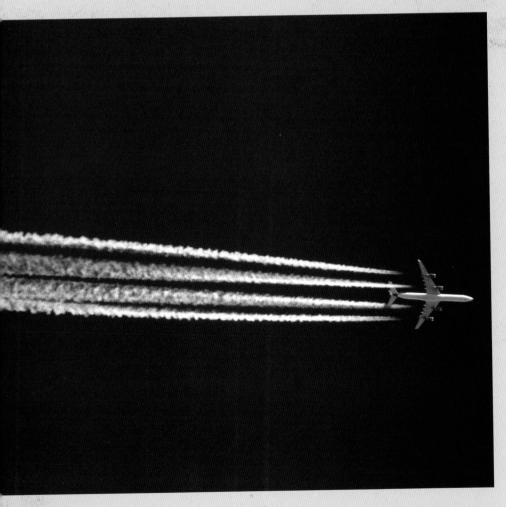

A tornado rips across the landscape. An American military report from 1996 described the possibility of using the weather as a weapon.

Owning the Weather in 2025' presented hypothetical strategies for how the American military could control the weather for war-fighting purposes – providing frightening possibilities with concerning names such as 'Decrease Comfort Level/Morale', 'Induce Drought', and 'Storm Enhancement'. The delivery system for these horror weapons would include 'clouds made of smart particles' and 'injection of chemical vapours'. It didn't take long for the nascent internet conspiracy movement to take these admittedly frightening concepts and develop its own theories about what the government was really doing. The long trails left by high-flying planes looked exactly what it might look like if the government was actually putting these tactics into action – despite an Air University report making it clear that as of its writing 'artificial weather technologies do not currently exist.'

Multiple government agencies leapt to action to debunk the growing conspiracy theory using fact sheets and research reports, but this only fuelled the fire of distrust, given that it was essentially the very people carrying out weather warfare trying to convince us that weather warfare was not real. Why wouldn't they? And so, the belief that they were spraying us in order to use our weather against us only grew stronger.

But like most conspiracy theories, even the alternate explanation for what contrails are (i.e. weather modification weapons) had alternate explanations. Some posited that the chemicals are actually a form of mind control, ensuring we're pliable to the brainwashing of the government and mass media and making us too lethargic to fight back. Others claim they're designed for general 'health erosion', making us sick so that Big Pharma can sell us cures for our man-made diseases – a perfect circle of decrepitude and greed. Blocking the sun, creating earthquakes, suppressing evolution, mass genetic modification of food, infesting our bodies with 'nano-fibres', and even carrying out genocide are all the supposed reasons for the government to spray our air with chemicals.

Some posited that the chemicals are actually a form of mind control, ensuring we're pliable to the brainwashing of the government and mass media and making us too lethargic to fight back.

Believers in the chemtrail conspiracy present a variety of pictures and videos as evidence that they claim are smoking guns. A few that have made the rounds on social media include multiple pictures of 'chemtrails tanks' inside aeroplanes (further research showed that these were only the ballast tanks used for testing the effects of passengers moving around during a flight), along with Photoshop-edited graphics and pictures of actual cloud formations that have simply been mislabelled.

THE SCIENCE OF CHEMTRAILS

In the case of chemtrails, the 'official story' seems the most plausible, based as it is on the bedrock of established science. Contrails form when hot gases from a jet engine hit the cold air of the upper atmosphere. The water vapour freezes very quickly after being emitted, combines with particles of dust or smoke, and forms a visible haze of microscopic ice crystals trailing behind the aeroplane. But the effect isn't instantaneous, which is why there's always a gap between the aeroplane and the contrail behind it.

Eventually, that trail of ice crystals either melts or smears as it dissipates – the reason why some contrails disappear fairly quickly, and others can linger for much longer, smearing into any number of shapes. It's entirely dependent on air temperature, humidity and wind. This effect is even visible on the ground. Just breathe out on a cold day. Hot water vapour leaves your mouth, and when it hits the cold air, it begins to freeze – hence the steam we breathe out when it's cold.

We've known about chemtrails for far longer than the conspiracy theory itself has been around. There are dozens of pictures of fleets of World War II bombers leaving contrails behind them, as well as newsreel footage of bucolic English country scenes dotted with the contrails of dogfighting aircraft above them during the Battle of Britain. Were they actually spraying weather modification chemicals on the enemy?

Even if there was an actual evil plot to use commercial jets to spray us with chemicals, using high-flying jets would be the least-efficient and least-effective way to carry it out. A thin chemical strand sprayed out by one plane miles above us would dissipate harmlessly and never reach us. You'd need to use fleets of crop dusters to spray people with chemicals in order to control our minds or infest us with fibres.

And who is flying these planes? Who is equipping them with these horrific chemicals? Who is giving the orders denoting what gets sprayed when and where? Are the passengers aware? The flight attendants?

Nobody seems to have any answers to these simple questions.

And if the 'chemicals' are meant to modify our weather, nobody has bothered to test the atmosphere for their effects. Because nobody agrees on what they are, there can't be tests for them. But just to be safe, a group of 77 actual atmospheric scientists, many of whom are experts in how chemicals interact with high altitude, dug through the 'evidence', then published a report in the high-impact, peer-reviewed journal *Environmental Research Letters.* Of those 77 scientists, 76 stated that they had found no evidence of what they defined as a 'secret large-scale atmospheric programme'. They deduced that everything we know about contrails can easily be explained by basic science and how the atmosphere works.

The chemtrail conspiracy is vague, nebulous and hard to prove. It will likely linger on the internet for a long time, but it is safe to say that we can rest assured that we aren't being poisoned, enslaved or threatened by contrails. They might look sinister, but they're really just science.

A sign warns about the dangers of chemtrails in Australia.

CERN

Located deep underneath the border between France and Switzerland lies a massive metal ring, full of pipes, wires, sensors and other sophisticated equipment. The nearly 27-kilometre loop, known as the Large Hadron Collider (LHC), is the most complex scientific instrument ever built, and was designed to replicate the conditions that existed in the universe in the moments after the Big Bang. But some believe its true purpose to be much darker – a way for scientists to touch the most evil forces known, and unleash pure terror on the people. Artificial earthquakes, portals to hell itself, directed energy weapons, mind control, alternate dimensions, microscopic black holes, even human sacrifice to ancient gods: all are suspected as the true purpose of the LHC, and its parent organization, CERN.

The size, scope and cost of the LHC all make it rife for conspiracy theories. It's a hugely expensive piece of scientific equipment that does things in the middle of nowhere that most people don't understand – giving us a clearer picture of the origin of the universe, as well as gigantic amounts of data to study. Through it all, though, misinformation and conspiracy theories persist, with fringe books and mainstream websites alike pushing out stories that are either misunderstandings of the work done there, or are simply false.

So what does CERN really do at the LHC? Is it a doorway to evil? Or a window into the birth of our reality?

The Large Hadron Collider at CERN has been blamed for everything from creating black holes to acting as an altar for human sacrifice to ancient gods.

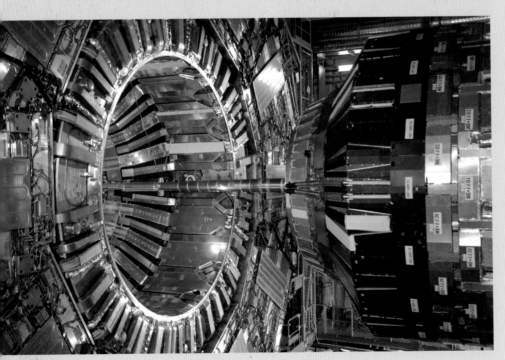

'TOTAL EXISTENCE FAILURE'

It's important to distinguish between CERN, the French acronym for the European Organization for Nuclear Research; and the Large Hadron Collider. Formed in 1954, CERN has 22 member states, has been awarded the Nobel Prize in Physics, and was the site of some of the earliest research for the world wide web. It's also where the Higgs boson, known as the 'God particle', was confirmed after decades of research. But the LHC captured the imaginations of both

The Globe of Science and Innovation at CERN.

the general public and the conspiracy theory community because of both its incredible cost and its purpose. It's designed to crash combined subatomic particles (known as 'hadrons') together at such speeds that they'll create new high-energy particles only known to exist at the dawn of time – shedding light on fundamental questions in physics and cosmology. As such, the LHC attracted conspiracy theories well before it was even activated. Fringe Christian theorists claimed that the LHC was actually opening a portal to hell, based on interpretations of biblical texts and strange looking clouds over the LHC site. The theory proved so popular that YouTube videos espousing it have racked up millions of views.

There were also fears that such meddling with the primal forces of nature might have devastating effects, including earthquakes, plasma storms and even destroying every molecule in the universe, a kind of 'total existence failure' only seen in apocalyptic science fiction. After all, nobody had previously attempted to recreate the energy of the dawn of the universe, so nobody could prove what would or wouldn't happen. The fact that the LHC was beset with delays, malfunctions and cost overruns even led some people to believe that there were higher powers trying to prevent the machine from being turned on. The most famous was a 2009 incident where a bird flew into the underground chamber and dropped a bit of bread into the electrical power system that ran the device's super-cooled magnets. Two esteemed scientists published a paper accusing the bird and other maladies of 'reverse chronological causation', – or that the LHC sent waves back in time causing it to try to turn itself off.

Despite the efforts of the time travelling bird, the LHC was indeed activated, firing its first particle collisions a few months later. And the

The statue of Shiva outside CERN was supposedly the site of ritual sacrifice, recorded in a video in 2016. The video was later revealed to be a hoax.

conspiracy theories have continued ever since. One popular theory is that the LHC has shifted humanity into an alternate dimension, and that the phenomenon of the 'Mandela Effect', where large masses remember events that never actually took place, is fragments of our original dimension reasserting themselves. There are also the usual accusations of CERN conducting time travel experiments, creating portals for alien spacecraft, trying to open 'quantum black holes' and summoning ancient demons foretold in the Revelation of John. Finally, there was the human sacrifice video that made the rounds in 2016, supposedly showing a candle-lit ceremony at the base of a statue of Shiva located on the grounds of CERN that ended with a ritual murder. While not all of these conspiracy theories could be true, couldn't at least a few? After all, how do you fake earthquakes and murder?

ALIENS AND WEASELS

Most of the theories about CERN and the LHC are based on a fundamental misunderstanding of physics, which is excusable, since particle physics is beyond most people's comprehension. It takes decades of training to understand concepts like the Higgs boson, pentaquarks and the strong and weak nuclear forces. But anyone can grab on to conspiracy theories like the destruction of the universe or a tunnel to hell. They require no training at all, just an imagination and preconceived biases. Because of the widespread appeal of CERN conspiracy theories, they're a pop culture stalwart. CERN and the LHC have been depicted on TV on *The Big Bang Theory*, *Ancient Aliens* and *Doctor Who*, along with the massively popular book *The Da Vinci Code*. They show CERN as unleashing horrific events like suicide epidemics, alien invasions and even mass zombification. Yet, paradoxically, there are viral videos made by CERN employees depicting exactly what the LHC does, and how amazing it is. CERN has also granted open access to its research to thousands of libraries, universities and scientific institutions.

While the 'human sacrifice' video turned out to be a prank, some of these conspiracy theories do at least have a grain of truth to them. The LHC was beset by problems and overspending, with its original opening, planned for November 2007, delayed for two years – culminating in the bread-bombing bird incident. The accidents didn't stop even after activation, as a weasel got into the electrical circuitry and caused a short that shut the LHC down briefly. But while there was no molecular collapse of the universe, there were mysterious earthquakes all over the world, from Italy and Switzerland to New Zealand, which CERN was forced to deny responsibility for; along with a mysterious seismic event in November 2018 where earthquake monitors detected 20 minutes of shaking with no apparent cause.

Pinning the blame for every one of these incidents, real and imagined alike, on CERN is just lazy conspiracy navel-gazing. No matter how fast subatomic particles are crashed together, they can't make earthquakes, control minds or open time portals. And even if they can, there will be a pause in them, because in November 2018, CERN announced the LHC would be shutting down for two years to perform upgrades and process the vast amount of data it had already collected. While it's possible that CERN simply wants to use the break to make more efficient hell portals and earthquake devices, it's more likely that they want to make sure that the LHC, already the coolest scientific instrument around, is even cooler for experiments to come. Trying to shed light on the beginning of the universe deserves nothing less than the most sophisticated machines available to humanity. And while they're at it, maybe they can do something to keep animals out.

An engineer works on the Large Hadron Collider. Seismic tremors across the world in 2016 forced CERN to issue a statement denying responsibility for them.

Index

Picture Credits

t = top, b = bottom, l = left, r = right

Alamy: 34 (Everett Collection), 73t (Gibson Green), 74b (Gado Images), 117 (The History Collection), 121 (Lukas Watschinger)

Bridgeman Images: 97 (British Library)

ESO: 100 (Tom Ruen/nagualdesign), 102 (E. Slawik)

Getty Images: 10 (Bettmann), 13 (National Archives – JFK), 19b (Afro American Newspapers/Gado), 20 (Bettmann), 21 (Bettmann), 23 (Michael Robinson Chavez/The Washington Post), 26 (Jim Rogash/WireImage), 27 (Consolidated News Pictures), 28 (Time Life Pictures/The LIFE Picture Collection), 29 (CQ Archive), 30, 33 (Jim Steinfeldt/Michael Ochs Archives), 36 (Sean Gallup), 39t (Adam Berry), 39b (Brooks Kraft), 41 (Hasan Tosun/Anadolu Agency), 58 (Bloomberg), 64 (Universal History Archive/UIG), 65 (ullstein bild), 66 (Maxim Marmur), 68 (Chris Ratcliffe/Bloomberg), 71 (Alex Wong), 75 (James D. Parcell/The Washington Post), 77 (Antonio Ribeiro/Gamma-Rapho), 87 (LSIS James Whittle/Australia Department of Defence), 90 (James Aylott/Hulton Archive), 91t (Mark Reinstein/Corbis), 92 (Alex Wong), 93t (Evan Agostini/Hulton Archive), 93b (Travis Heying/AFP), 98b (Kent Photo News/Express/Hulton Archive), 99 (Hyoung Chang/The Denver Post), 101b (David Maxwell/AFP), 107 (Andy King/Sygma), 113 (George Panagakis/Pacific Press/LightRocket), 125 (Francis Demange/Gamma-Rapho)

NASA: 7

National Archives and Records Administration, USA: 16, 116

Shutterstock: 8 (Vic Hinterlang), 17 (amadeustx), 24r (ES James), 32 (Fabio Diena), 35, 42, 43, 46, 50, 51, 55 (mark reinstein), 56 (Michael Fitzsimmons), 63 (Adrin Shamsudin), 67 (evenfh), 69 (Sean Pavone), 73b (Martin Good), 76, 88, 94 (Randy Hume), 103, 104 (Dominionart), 108, 110, 111 (David Cohen 156), 112, 114, 122 (D-Visions)

Wellcome Collection: 72

Wikimedia Commons: 6, 12, 14, 15, 18, 19t, 24l, 25, 38, 44t, 44b, 45, 47, 48t, 48b, 49, 52t, 52b, 54, 56, 61, 62, 74t, 78, 79, 80, 82, 83, 84, 85, 86, 89t, 89b, 91b, 95, 96, 101, 106, 109, 118, 123, 124